B
Charles Dickens

Brief Lives:
Charles Dickens

Melissa Valiska Gregory and
Melisa Klimaszewski

ET REMOTISSIMA PROPE

Brief Lives
Published by Hesperus Press Limited
4 Rickett Street, London SW6 1RU
www.hesperuspress.com

First published by Hesperus Press Limited, 2008

Designed and typeset by Fraser Muggeridge studio
Printed in Jordan by Jordan National Press

ISBN: 1-84391-901-X
ISBN13: 978-1-84391-901-8

Contents

Introduction

How to enter the life of Charles Dickens? With his fairly unremarkable birth into a modest middle-class family in Portsmouth in 1812? With his death as a celebrated novelist in 1870? Or perhaps with his writing? His novels? His journalism? His public readings? His cast of thousands? His famous depiction of urban life in Victorian London, the city that shaped him? Or with his afterlife, evident in countless novel, stage, film and television adaptations of his work? Opening any one of these doors on Dickens' life changes our view, from the boy who aspired to success to the celebrated author whose work not only captured his contemporary culture, but also continues to reverberate throughout our own. As a writer with a rich and complicated personal life and a tremendous artistic legacy, there is no obvious beginning to Dickens.

The world into which he was born was similarly complex, characterised by remarkable social, political and cultural developments. The year of Dickens' birth witnessed the War of 1812, the madness of George III, Luddite riots in the north of England and Napoleon's final efforts to conquer Europe. By his death, Queen Victoria had been on the throne for over thirty-three years, the Industrial Revolution had transformed commercial production and the middle classes across Europe, and the British Empire was well on its way to covering one-quarter of the globe. In 1812, the primary mode of travel was the coach. In 1870, the year of his death, it was the railway. Over the course of Dickens' lifetime, the population of London exploded from one million to five, and many of its substantial rural spaces turned into vast urban slums. Three important reform acts (1832, 1867, 1884) enfranchised a whole new class of voters. A rising middle class demanded more servants, and the total population of English men and women in service grew to 15.9%. Women agitated for increased financial and political independence, eventually making their way into universities and earning the right to keep their own wages earned after marriage. Public libraries flourished, and basic literacy rates steadily rose. Many of Dickens' tastes and literary habits were formed before Victoria ascended the throne in 1837, and his fiction often looks back ten, twenty, even fifty years into the past. Yet he is often considered the quintessential Victorian novelist, and his major work occurred during her reign. Thinking of Dickens within this fluid and shifting social context may help to explain his wonderful dynamism. Dickens made an indelible mark on the novel as we now know it, but his work, like his life, resists tidy formulations.

In this biography, we attempt to sketch the arc of Dickens' personal and professional life without losing sight of its irresolvable tensions or conflicts. On one hand, we hope to make his life coherent within this brief framework. We use a chronological organisation that touches on his life's major events and, by necessity, have minimised certain friends, some family members, and an extended discussion of the social context that influenced his work. We have also prioritised the familiar writing, particularly his novels, at the expense of many of his articles, speeches, plays, verse and short fiction. We hope that this skeleton approach will facilitate a working knowledge of Dickens while at the same time encouraging further reading of his life and his work. On the other hand, we remain cognisant of the messiness of all life writing. The main way in which we can now come to know Dickens is through the writing he left behind – not only his fiction, but also his thousands of letters. These documents offer invaluable insights, but they were, like all his writing, occasions for performance. They are not always straightforward or unembellished accounts of events or even his mood at the time. Hence, we occasionally pause to consider the textual nature of Dickens: the implications of his choice of phrasing or the timing of his letters. Sometimes, we offer more than one interpretation of events, highlighting the indefinite nature of any biographical work. For ease of reading, we do not use notes, but we have included many of our sources in the appendix of further suggested readings. Whenever quoting Dickens' letters, we have included a month and year, or just enough information to ensure that an interested reader may track down the entire text.

Ultimately, this volume of the Brief Lives series aims to capture some of the extraordinary richness of Dickens, from his rather unassuming childhood to his death as one of the world's most famous authors.

– Melissa Valiska Gregory and Melisa Klimaszewski

Beginnings
1812–32

Tiny Tim. Oliver Twist. David Copperfield. Today, we instantly recognise the names of some of Dickens' more famous fictional children as well as the phrases that are famously attached to them. 'God Bless Us, Every One'. 'Please, sir, I want some more'. 'Whether I shall turn out to be the hero of my own life...'. Dickens' vivid depiction of these child characters has imbued them with an unusually long cultural afterlife, and he continues to be known as a writer who renders childhood feelings and experiences with powerful intensity. His gift for portraying childhood can be attributed in part to the ready presence of his own childhood, kept always near the surface of his consciousness. Even as an adult, Dickens could at any moment turn a corner and come face to face with his former self, as if it had been waiting there the whole time. In 'Travelling Abroad', an essay written when he was forty-eight, Dickens describes a chance encounter with a 'very queer small boy' on a walk in Chatham who turns out to be none other than the young Charles Dickens. The two Dickenses, young and old, proceed to have a conversation about a house at the top of a hill. The younger Dickens admires it wistfully from a distance. The older Dickens, it turns out, owns it. This odd little story might be interpreted as an inspirational narrative of hard work rewarded: the man grows up to acquire what his boyhood self could only dream of. Yet what stands out in Dickens' description is not his current, worldly self, but his plaintive nostalgia for his former self: the 'queer small boy' who cannot imagine that he would ever own such a wonderful house. Despite his tremendous professional success and personal accomplishments, Dickens persistently imagined himself as a defenceless and frail outsider. His many friendships, his bustling household of children and his considerable self-confidence in his own professional abilities: nothing could shake Dickens' profound sense of childhood vulnerability, which he could access at any time. To begin a biography of Charles Dickens with his own childhood, then, is to acknowledge that for Dickens, childhood was never far away.

What was that childhood? Charles was born in Portsmouth on 7th February 1812 to John and Elizabeth Dickens. John was a warm, generous and loquacious man from relatively humble origins. His mother had been a servant. His father, William Dickens, was the steward for a large hall in Chester, and his employers helped to pay for John's education. They also ultimately helped John to obtain his post as a clerk at the Navy Pay Office in 1805. John Dickens met his wife, Elizabeth Barrow, through her brother, Thomas, a fellow clerk. Elizabeth was bright, lively and educated, with a natural gift for mimicry that she passed on to her son Charles. She married John at the age of eighteen and ultimately bore him eight children, two of whom died in infancy. Large families were not uncommon in the Victorian period, but the number of children in the Dickens household contributed to a general strain on the family resources. John Dickens' income never quite accommodated his large family or his aspirations to bourgeois respectability. Consequently, Charles grew up in an atmosphere that he would later describe as genteel poverty. This early financial instability helped to form Dickens' fierce work ethic and the professional ambition that characterised his adult life.

In 1817, the Navy transferred John Dickens to Chatham with his family. There are no photographs, of course, to show us what the young Charles looked like at the age of five, but later pictures suggest that he was fair, with delicate features and large brown eyes inherited from his mother. Dickens recalls being a self-conscious boy who was more of an observer than a participant, preferring to watch others at play rather than joining in. Yet he appears to have made friends at school easily and to have been outgoing and lively. He was an avid reader. He devoured litera-ture, reading all the novels in his parents' modest library. He adored Tobias Smollett's *Humphrey Clinker* (1771) and later wove elements of the picaresque tradition into his own fiction, send-ing his heroes travelling back and forth across the English coun-tryside. He also loved reading recent translations of *The Arabian Nights*, a collection of Arabic tales dating from the eighth cen-tury, and even wrote his own youthful version of one of the tragic *Tales of the Genii* entitled *Misnar, the Sultan of India*. Although an experiment with tragedy may have been one of his first written pieces, as a child, Dickens was better known for his sense of humour. Quick-witted and with a natural gift for show-manship, his father encouraged him to give comic performances and to sing rowdy songs on tabletops (he later ruefully recalled that he must have been insufferable).

Dickens' cousin James Lamert was the first to take him to the theatre, and, at the young age of six, Dickens was more than sus-ceptible to the intense thrills of the stage. He said that 'his young heart leapt with terror as the wicked King Richard, struggling for life against the virtuous Richmond, backed up and bumped against the box in which he was'. Of *Macbeth*, he wryly recalled, 'good King Duncan couldn't rest in his grave, but was constantly coming out of it, and calling himself somebody else'. Dickens retained his keen awareness of the pleasures and potential foibles of theatre throughout his life, ultimately becoming an expert at creating dramatically compelling literary moments that veer toward ridiculous (like the doubled parts in the *Macbeth* he had seen so long ago) but pull back just in time to preserve their comic effect without becoming ridiculous themselves. He not only directed and starred in many private theatricals, but also –

incisively but not unkindly – spoofed unsophisticated productions in many of his novels, including his famously over-the-top depiction of Mr Wopsle's *Hamlet* in *Great Expectations* (1860–1).

By the time Charles was ten, there were five children in the Dickens family, and the household debt was mounting. In order to live more cheaply, John Dickens moved the family from Chatham to the much grubbier neighbourhood of Camden Town. Why the Dickens family's financial troubles were so persistent remains somewhat unclear even today. There has been some speculation that John Dickens may have gambled, but no evidence has been discovered to support this theory. He clearly failed to develop responsible financial habits or coping skills. It may be, more simply, that a large family with bourgeois sensibilities could not muster the financial discipline to live affordably on a naval clerk's low to middling salary. John Dickens tended to buy goods on credit thinking that he would have the resources to pay for them later, but he never did. To combat their rising debt, Elizabeth decided to open a school for which the family rented an expensive house on Gower Street North. Dickens recalled being impressed with a showy brass plate for the door announcing the establishment. Unfortunately, however, not a single student enrolled, and the school was a complete failure.

Young Charles was devastated by the move to Camden. At Chatham he had friends, but in Camden he was lonely and isolated. In a solitary attempt to entertain himself, he wandered daily about London, beginning a life-long intimacy with the city's streets. James Lamert compassionately built him a miniature theatre to play with, and Dickens spent many hours inventing plays. The image of young Dickens playing alone with a toy theatre points toward a tension that structured Dickens' later life between his more gregarious impulses on one hand and his sense of himself as a solitary being on the other. Dickens spent much of his life yearning for the extroverted and companionable world that he found so readily in the theatre. He was always eager for friends, bustle and collaborative projects. At the same time, Dickens also loved playing all the parts: the role of the playwright, the director and the entire cast. His childhood theatre may have been lonely by necessity, but his need to control his professional world never disappeared. Many future instances show Dickens inviting a friend to collaborate on a project only to rewrite his or her work or, as with some of the Christmas numbers, to exclude that work entirely from reprints. These professional dynamics, of course, were a long way from the ten-year-old Dickens alone with his toy theatre. Indeed, one of the most formative moments of his childhood had yet to occur.

In February of 1824, Dickens' father was arrested for debt. He was placed in a 'sponging house', a halfway house for debtors that allowed them more time to try to pay off their bills. John Dickens, however, failed to make timely reparations and was sent to the Marshalsea prison between 20th February and 28th May 1824. In a desperate effort to keep their house, the Dickens family pawned most of their personal items, including Charles' beloved books and most of their furniture. While John waited in prison for his situation to be resolved, the rest of the family lived in the two parlours of their empty Gower Street house along with a few chairs and some beds. In April, Elizabeth and the youngest children were forced to move into the Marshalsea with John. It was not uncommon for entire families to live in debtors' prison (a scenario that Dickens exaggerated over thirty years later in *Little Dorrit*), but Dickens himself did not live there with his family. His favourite sister Fanny stayed at the Royal Academy of Music, where she was a pupil, while Charles moved in with a friend of the family. This sudden domestic instability – the grim household circumstances, the break-up of the family, the humiliation of debtors' prison – would surely be enough to trouble any sensitive boy. And Fanny's success during this period – she won the Academy's silver medal for a recital in June of 1824 – further amplified Charles' own sense of loss and thwarted ambition. Although he and Fanny were close and shared the hard walk to and from the prison together, her achievement shamed him because he was sent to work. James Lamert, the same cousin who had built Dickens his toy theatre, had recently taken a position as the chief manager of his cousin George's boot-blacking warehouse. Lamert tried to help improve the family's situation by volunteering to employ Charles at the warehouse for six or seven shillings per week. Virtually on the eve of his father's arrest, John and Elizabeth decided to remove Charles from school. They took Lamert up on his offer and sent the boy to Warren's Blacking, 30 Hungerford Stairs, the Strand, where he worked throughout his father's imprisonment.

What was it like for the twelve-year-old Dickens to work at Warren's Blacking? His daily routine was fairly straightforward. He no longer lived with his family, but he was not wholly deprived of them. He found new lodgings close to the Marshalsea, and he and Fanny ate breakfast with the rest of the Dickenses in prison each morning. He would then walk to work for a ten-hour day and return again to the Marshalsea for supper. He was back in his rented room by nine o'clock every night. He and Fanny also spent Sundays in the Marshalsea. But breakfasts and evenings with his family could not protect the young boy from the extreme distress that being sent to work provoked. Warren's Blacking was neither the worst nor the best example of industrial working conditions in the early nineteenth century. In Dickens' own description, however, it was a gothic horror show. The warehouse was 'a crazy, tumble-down old house' in a dirty and fetid area of London, right next to the Thames. Its floors were rotting and its lower levels were crowded with rats, whose 'squeaking and scuffling' could be heard 'coming up the stairs at all times'. Dickens was assigned the repetitive, monotonous task of pasting labels onto jars of boot blacking. He covered the pots with oil, then with blue paper, tied them with a string and clipped the paper, he said, 'close and neat, all round, until it looked as smart as a pot of ointment from an apothecary's shop'. He then pasted printed labels over the paper. Dickens performed this task day in, day out, often sitting in the front window of the warehouse for light.

The young boy desperately missed his family and school. He felt disconnected from the other workers, with whom he was cordial but never overly friendly. Another boy working there – Bob Fagin, whose surname Dickens later borrowed for *Oliver Twist* (1837–9) – taught him the finer points of his job, but the boys were too different to form a strong bond. James Lamert had arranged to tutor Dickens during his lunch hour, but this plan gradually fell by the wayside. The work was dull, the environment oppressive and the duration of his labour indefinite. His parents had always claimed middle-class status; Dickens had expected the same. Sitting on display in the window of the factory, he felt as if he had been woefully miscast in the wrong role. His father's incarceration painfully exploded all sense of domestic security, and he felt betrayed by his parents, who seemed not to care about how he felt. The job burdened him with adult responsibilities before he was ready. He was unable to manage his meagre funds, for instance, and would often buy the stale pastry on sale at confectioners' shops on his way to work, leaving himself nothing to eat for the rest of the day. In a child's effort to achieve some measure of financial security, he attempted to manage his money by dividing it equally into small wrapped parcels, labelled with each day of the week. These rather dismal efforts did not prevent him from going hungry on a regular basis, and he would prowl the street to stare longingly at shop windows with lavish displays of food. Dickens' feelings about his job were a complicated mix of shame, anguish and acute vulnerability.

Long after his employment was over, he never forgot the blacking warehouse. He never spoke of it to anyone until 1847, when he recounted it to his friend and eventual first biographer, John Forster. Forster had heard brief mention of the blacking factory from a mutual acquaintance. When he asked Dickens about the episode, Dickens dramatically bowed his head and refused to answer. He did not mention it again until weeks later, when he claimed that the time spent in the blacking factory continued to haunt him. Dickens later folded his autobiographical notes into *David Copperfield* (1849–50). But he also sent an account of it in writing to Forster, who preserved it in Volume I of his biography, *The Life of Charles Dickens* (1872–4). Although Dickens later kept a brief diary of daily events, this is the only piece of autobiography that he ever produced. The flavour of his boyhood misery emerges even in a short extract:

> No words can express the secret agony of my soul as I sunk into this companionship; compared these every day associates with those of my happier childhood; and felt my early hopes of growing up to be a learned and distinguished man, crushed in my breast. The deep remembrance of the sense I had of being utterly neglected and hopeless; of the shame I felt in my position; of the misery it was to my young heart to believe that, day by day, what I had learned, and thought, and delighted in, and raised my fancy and my emulation up by, was passing away from me, never to be brought back any more; cannot be written. My whole nature was so penetrated with the grief and humiliation of such considerations, that even now, famous and caressed and happy, I often forget in my dreams that I have a dear wife and children; even that I am a man; and wander desolately back to that time of my life.

Biographers of Dickens' life eagerly seized on the blacking warehouse episode, and, today, encyclopedia entries, websites and thumbnail sketches in editions of Dickens' novels all feature it prominently as a formative experience. Even people who know very little about his life are cognisant of this event and can cite its influence on some of Dickens' most important fictional motifs and personal choices. Is the blacking warehouse the key to Dickens' work, the trauma that motivates his professional success and explains his personal failures? The source of both his ferocious self-discipline and his drive to succeed? Dickens' reluctance to mention the episode suggests how deeply it distressed him, and specific images and feelings from this period of his life assemble with undeniable persistence in his fiction. Prisons and boot blacking appear regularly, as do the twinned themes of guilt and secrecy. More generally, the residual feelings from the blacking warehouse could explain the sheer intensity of Dickens' sympathetic portraits of children who lack control over their own lives.

It is worth remembering, however, that the fragment of auto-biography where Dickens describes the blacking warehouse is also a highly crafted account. He says there are 'no words' to describe his feelings even while he manages to deliver a polished narrative. In lieu of any other substantial first-hand accounts of the blacking warehouse, it is natural to assign this brief autobi-ographical writing tremendous authority and to take it as the closest thing we have to Dickens telling his own story: a kind of unvarnished, unmediated account. Yet this seems unlikely, since there are few such accounts in Dickens' writing, and he rarely lost an opportunity for rhetorical performance. Even the briefest of his letters reveal a keen awareness of self-presentation, and Dickens went out of his way to control his image in print. In 1847, when he presented the story to Forster, he was well aware that anything he wrote might be made public, passed on, or even reprinted. The retroactive prominence assigned to the blacking factory, then, is partially of Dickens' own making. He chose to exert authorial control over this aspect of his legacy as he did with few other moments from his life. Surely he was truthful in his memory of himself as miserable and vulnerable during this period, but his account also deflects any potential class snobbery against an author who had worked in a factory instead of going to school. If he had publicised the blacking factory episode to authorise his depiction of working-class life in his later fiction, laying claim to it as something that he had experienced first-hand, then it might have diminished his social status. Dickens' fiction may have championed the working classes and the poor, but he always adopted a middle-class perspective.

Hence, there is every reason to attend to this important moment from Dickens' childhood, but also to be wary of the pat formulation that it accounts for everything else in his world.

On 28th May 1824, John Dickens was finally released under the Insolvent Debtors Act, which required his family to undergo a humiliating assessment to prove that their personal belongings did not add up to more than £20. He had spent fourteen weeks in prison and then received permission to retire from the Navy Pay Office on a fixed pension because of his persistent kidney and urinary problems. The family moved into a new house. Charles continued to work at Warren's Blacking, but in 1825, his father withdrew him after a quarrel with James Lamert. The reasons for the quarrel remain unknown, but Dickens later speculated that his father was humiliated by seeing him working in the window. Elizabeth Dickens tried to mend the quarrel and succeeded in persuading Lamert to ask her son back to the factory, much to Charles' dismay. He never fully forgave her for failing to understand his distress. His father, however, refused to allow it, and Charles was re-enrolled in school.

The Wellington House Academy on Hampstead Road was a relatively well-respected but not especially rigorous school where Dickens delightedly made friends his own age for the first time in a while. He and his schoolfellows were a rowdy bunch. They played street games, kept canaries and white mice in their desks, staged small theatricals in toy theatres and read penny dreadfuls. Dickens happily reprised his role as comic performer, entertaining his friends with songs such as 'The Cat Meat's Man'. It was a welcome respite from the pain of the blacking warehouse. The family's financial difficulties continued, however, and even though he lived with his parents for the next several years, Dickens' boyhood was virtually at an end.

In 1827, Elizabeth Dickens persuaded a solicitor named Edward Blackmore to employ Charles for the salary of fifteen shillings a week. He left school permanently and entered the working world as a law clerk. Dickens was fifteen and still small for his age, but he was determined and scrappy. On his first day of work, he dressed boldly, possibly to offset his physical vulnerability. He wore a blue jacket and a military-style cap rakishly set askew. While he was out delivering papers, an older boy, irritated by his jaunty air, knocked the cap off his head. They fought. Dickens returned to the office with a black eye but undaunted. With this kind of lively confidence, he quickly made friends in the office. He was particularly close with a fellow clerk named Thomas Potter, with whom he frequented minor theatrical productions and amateur private theatres, where he saw most of Shakespeare's plays.

One year later, Dickens moved to the firm of Charles Molloy. His friend Thomas Mitton also worked there, but, while Mitton ultimately became a successful lawyer who served as Dickens' own solicitor for over twenty years, Dickens had other plans. Perhaps inspired by his father, who had begun writing occasional short pieces for the newspapers, Dickens decided to pursue a career in journalism. He set about teaching himself shorthand. It was no easy task. With one of the standard manuals as his only teacher, it required hours of practice. Dickens worked intensely to accomplish in three months what others often took three years to learn. At the same time, he spent hours reading. He haunted the British Museum reading room and also joined a circulating library, absorbing as much literature as he could in the little spare time he had left. This self-education was an impressively wide-ranging substitute for any formal training he might have received at school.

Dickens left Ellis and Blackmore at the end of November 1828, two months shy of his seventeenth birthday. He was determined to hire himself out as a freelance reporter in Doctors' Commons, London's ecclesiastical court. By the time he was nineteen, Dickens had managed to find employment with several papers. One of the first to hire him was *The Mirror of Parliament*, a paper recently founded by Dickens' uncle, John Henry Barrow. It was devoted to transcribing Parliamentary proceedings, and Barrow hired Dickens as a regular member of the reporting staff. He arrived in the press gallery just in time to witness the important debates over the first Reform Bill of 1832. This act radically reapportioned Parliamentary representation and extended voting rights to any man with a home worth at least £10. It also purged rotten boroughs and sought more accurate representation, thereby doubling the electorate and granting one man out of every five the opportunity to vote. Dickens himself ultimately benefited from this change. His first-hand observation of the debates, moreover, fundamentally influenced his political sensibilities, especially his commitment to the poor.

Dickens was also hired as a general reporter by a new sevenpenny evening newspaper, *The True Sun*. From the moment he accepted the position, he worked steadily. The schedule was exhausting: he frequently attended midnight Parliamentary debates, for which he was paid overtime, and travelled regularly to cover elections in all kinds of inclement weather. He recalled later that in travelling back and forth to London, he had been overturned in almost every sort of vehicle there was. Necessity often forced him to finish his articles on the road on the way back to London, looking over his notes as the coach bounced and swayed, splashing mud through the open windows. But Dickens loved the work. 'I have never forgotten the fascination of that old pursuit,' he told Forster. 'The pleasure that I used to feel in the rapidity and dexterity of its exercise has never faded from my breast.' Dickens' work as a reporter paid off in his literary career, training his memory, sharpening his already keen eye for detail and ear for dialogue, and forming the basis for the satirical view of contemporary politics that so often surfaces in his work. Finally, Dickens' employment as a reporter marked the last break from his boyhood. He still lived with the Dickenses in 1832, but he soon found his own lodgings and eventually took on the role of helping his family through their ongoing financial difficulties. By the time he was twenty, the 'queer small boy' had launched himself successfully into the adult world.

Boz
1833–9

Even the intense demands of Dickens' Parliamentary reporting could not quell his incredible energy. Both to alleviate the monotony of reporting and to supplement his salary, he began to experiment with other kinds of writing: sketches and brief stories. Over the course of seven years, Dickens would move from newspaper reporting to writing short fictional sketches, plays and, ultimately, fully fledged novels. He also continued to work as a journalist but shifted his position from reporter to editor, assuming the role of editor-in-chief of one of the major new journals of the period. Having begun the decade of the 1830s as an unknown reporter, he concluded it having written a novel that engaged some of the most urgent problems of the period, establishing his role not only as a writer of fiction but also as an agent for moral and social reform.

Dickens published his first sketch, 'A Dinner at Poplar Walk', in *The Monthly Magazine* in December of 1833. 'I am so dreadfully nervous,' he wrote to his friend Henry Kolle on the third of that month, 'that my hand shakes to such an extent as to prevent my writing a word legibly.' The editor of *The Monthly* liked the story and eventually requested more writing. The *London Weekly Magazine* liked it so much that they reprinted it without Dickens' or the magazine's permission. Such unauthorised reprints both annoyed and flattered Dickens, but when they continued to plague his career, the flattery gave way to increased irritation.

Dickens continued to contribute funny sketches to *The Monthly Magazine* throughout 1833 despite the journal's policy of not paying for these short pieces. The earliest ones were published anonymously, but, by August of that year, he began to publish under the pseudonym of 'Boz', after his nickname for his seven-year-old brother Augustus. (He called the boy 'Moses' after Oliver Goldsmith's son in the 1766 *The Vicar of Wakefield*. Augustus' inability to pronounce the word transformed it to 'Boses', which eventually diminished to 'Boz'.) As is true of much 'anonymous' work from this period, the identity of Boz was more of an open secret than a true disguise: Dickens' friends, family and fellow reporters all knew that he was the author, and he thoroughly enjoyed the attention he received for his work.

Dickens' style for these first pieces brought something new to the literary scene. His journalism training clearly influenced the subject matter and rhythms of his early sketches, but he also tended to parody journalistic conventions of the time, many of which had been inherited from the eighteenth century. He lampooned their grandiloquence and softened their satirical edge, unafraid of sentiment as he tried to inspire strong feelings of pity or sympathy in his readers. Dickens adapted the typical verbosity of contemporary journalistic writing to his own purposes, transforming its long-winded style into his trademark comically complex sentences. Even this brief excerpt from his first published piece, which describes the fussy blandness of a forty-something bachelor named Mr Augustus Minns, contains the hallmarks of the writing style for which Dickens is now famous:

> He usually wore a brown frock-coat without a wrinkle, light inexplicables without a spot, a neat neckerchief with a remarkably neat tie, and boots without a fault; moreover, he always carried a brown silk umbrella with an ivory handle.

This exhaustive description is rhythmically driven by the pulse of a recurring word: 'without, without, without'. Densely clustered repeated adjectives ('neat' and 'brown') are intensified even further: the tie is not only neat, but 'remarkably neat'. Dickens even humorously turns 'inexplicable' into a noun, and he may well have been the first person to coin the word (the *Oxford English Dictionary* cites this very sketch). Such a fleeting analysis of a short excerpt only begins to touch upon the complexities of Dickens' style, but it illuminates the impressive self-assurance of his youthful work, which exhibits elements we now immediately recognise as 'Dickensian'.

These sketches also drew upon what Dickens knew. In the pieces he published over the next three years for *The Morning Chronicle*, *The Evening Chronicle* and *Bell's Life in London*, he explores almost every corner of the city, ranging from the poorest gin shop in the slums to the idyllic middle-class home. Pawnbrokers' shops, ladies' societies, dancing academies, hospitals and prisons all materialise within the pages of this work. So do feelings and impressions from his family life. In the case of 'A Dinner at Poplar Walk', he depicts an aspiring lower-middle-class family attempting to secure the financial fortune of their son by pandering unsuccessfully to his wealthy bachelor godfather. Their vulgar pretensions – an overstuffed garden, Cupid statues flanking the front door, a silver buttoned suit worn by the young son – resonate with Dickens' personal life at the moment. The great efforts he made to establish himself were constantly jeopardised by his parents, who continued to teeter precariously on the edge of financial ruin throughout this time of his life. The Dickens family was evicted for defaulting on their rent in their Somers Town home in 1827 and moved several times to avoid creditors. In November of 1831, John Dickens was once again declared an insolvent debtor and ultimately arrested three years later for an outstanding bill. Many of Dickens' early stories feature similarly improvident individuals and families. In this work, however, Dickens tends to convert any anxiety he may have felt about poverty into humour.

For all his success with his initial pieces, Dickens was by no means committed to becoming a full-time writer at this stage of his career. He continued to be attracted to the theatre, which he later claimed he attended almost every night for three years. He practised the movements and gestures common to the nineteenth-century stage for hours at a time and taught himself techniques for memorising lines from a standard theatrical manual. In March of 1832, the year just prior to the publication of his first short story, he boldly wrote to the manager of Covent Garden Theatre to request an audition. The manager agreed, and he arranged for Dickens to audition in front of him and Charles Kemble, one of the period's most famous actors. Fanny promised to accompany him. When the day arrived, however, Dickens fell ill with a terrible cold that inflamed his entire face. He wrote to say that he would reapply next season, but he never did. If Dickens had auditioned successfully, his writing career might have been entirely rerouted, but it is difficult to say whether his acting would have achieved the same kind of cultural prominence eventually secured by his fiction. His later private performances and public readings demonstrated tremendous energy and personal charisma, but he was not a typical leading man and might have found himself relegated to minor roles. By contrast, in private performances cast with friends and family, Dickens could shine not only as an actor, but also as a stage manager. This may explain why he never re-auditioned and why, in the next year, he plunged the entire family into a series of private theatricals at their home in Bentinck Street. Dickens ambitiously selected a light operetta, an interlude and a farce. Much like the small boy who used to play alone with his miniature theatre, Dickens supervised every level of the show: directing, acting (assigning the starring roles to himself), staging and costuming. The plays were successfully performed on 23rd April 1833 in honour of Shakespeare's birthday, and others followed.

Dickens' sudden commitment to private theatricals may also have helped him to cope with the recent conclusion of his first love affair. In 1830, when he was just eighteen, Dickens fell in love with a young woman named Maria Beadnell and courted her for the next two years. The daughter of a respectable middle-class bank manager, Maria was petite and pretty, with dark curls and lively eyes. She was also conventionally accomplished and would play the harp with her sister Anne while Dickens listened with rapt attention. Well aware of her charms, she flirted decorously with several admirers. By 1831, she and Dickens had achieved a certain intimacy, exchanging letters and small tokens through mutual friends such as Henry Kolle and Mary Anne ('Marianne') Leigh, Maria's best friend. The depth of Maria's commitment to Dickens is difficult to gauge. She obviously favoured him for a while, but she seems to have been less serious about him than he was about her. The Beadnells treated him cordially, despite Mrs Beadnell's inability to remember his name (she called him 'Mr Dickin'). Yet it is also likely that her parents were wary of a potential son-in-law whose father was a persistent debtor, regardless of Dickens' own obvious efforts to escape the taint of financial irresponsibility. Some time in late 1831, they sent Maria away to Paris, ostensibly to finish her education but perhaps also to separate her from Dickens. When she returned, their relationship was never quite the same. Over the next two years, she increasingly rebuffed his advances and ultimately hurt his feelings in the extreme by telling him at his own coming-of-age party in February of 1833 that she thought of him as a boy. Between March and May of 1833, Dickens pushed for further commitment, but the relationship finally collapsed.

It is worth attending to the character of Dickens' first love because it illuminates personal dynamics that continued throughout his life. Although many of his mistakes may be attributed to the rashness characteristic of youthful romance, the relationship's failure cannot be reduced solely to a matter of immaturity. Dickens' attachment to Maria reveals the more unsettled, needy aspects of his personality that consistently affected his major relationships. His letters from the period of his courtship suggest that he was highly, often overly, sensitive. He would quickly adopt a posture of wounded self-righteousness with each small slight, refusing to accept any partial responsibility and holding everyone to high and sometimes unrealistic standards of conduct. Maria's friend Mary Anne, for instance, insisted on interfering with their relationship, provoking disagreements between the couple and suggesting that Dickens was instead courting her. (Maybe she herself was interested in him.) Instead of responding to her unwelcome meddling with humour or ignoring her altogether, Dickens rose to her baiting, sending hurt and angry letters of protest. His final letters to Maria also focus on his grievances, dwelling less upon the loss of her affection and more upon the nature of her treatment of him. He repeatedly criticises her 'heartless indifference' while simultaneously professing that his own behaviour is irreproachable. 'I have done nothing that I could say would be very likely to hurt you,' he wrote on 18th March. 'If (I can hardly believe it possible) I have said any thing which can have that effect I can only ask you to place yourself for a moment in my situation...'

Dickens would make such claims throughout his life. To his credit, he would often scrupulously review his own conduct in social conflicts with high emotional stakes. But his self-scrutiny almost always resulted in a heightened sense of his own blamelessness rather than a more nuanced understanding of his shared responsibility. He persistently expected others to be as alert to the prospect of hurting his feelings as he was to the prospect of hurting theirs. While his heightened awareness to others' moods and potential reactions made him a loyal and sympathetic friend, his sensitivity also left him prone to emotional injury. Combined with a tendency to idealise women – his desire for a mate who was enchanting, angelic and perfectly domestic – it is not surprising that his affair with Maria dissolved, or that the nature of this break-up foreshadows some of his later domestic difficulties. Dickens' rather cruel caricature of an older Maria Beadnell as the fat and frivolous Flora Finching in Little Dorrit (1855–7) suggests that he never quite forgave her for having wounded him.

At least Dickens had other companions to help counter the loss of his first love. In his early twenties, Dickens began to form important friendships with other men: fellow law clerk Thomas Mitton, who later became Dickens' solicitor; fellow reporter Thomas Beard; and Henry Kolle, a bank clerk acquainted with the Beadnells. With his male friends, Dickens converted the social sensitivity that may have contributed to the dissolution of his relationship with Maria into one of his greatest assets. He tended to his friendships carefully, never taking them for granted. When Kolle became engaged to Maria's older sister in 1833, for instance, he refused to let his own disappointed feelings sour their relationship. Kolle and his wife were the first to read 'A Dinner at Poplar Walk', and Dickens begged to be made godfather of their first child. When Thomas Mitton purchased a third share in the law firm of Smithson and Dunn in 1838, Dickens stood surety for £1,050. In turn, Dickens relied upon and trusted his friends, occasionally borrowing small sums (always promptly repaid) and humbly requesting assistance from them when his family fell into financial difficulties. When John Dickens was once again arrested for debt, Dickens turned to Tom Beard, asking him to visit his father in prison when Dickens could not get away from work.

Dickens not only sustained some of these friendships for decades, but also developed a lifelong appreciation of the pleasures of the bachelor lifestyle. It became one of his habits to cultivate groups of male friends who would gather to enjoy pubs, clubs, restaurants and the theatre. Dickens happily provided entertainment for the group. Neither wealthy nor powerful in these days, his primary resource was comedy. The boy who used to stand on tabletops and sing comic songs was never far from reach. His letters from 1832 show him regularly inviting his friends out to 'knock up a song or two' or 'take a Glass of Punch and a Cigar' at home. He asked 'a Brother or two' to celebrate his twenty-second birthday with 'a friendly quadrille' and included his friends in invitations to celebrate Christmas

Day. Ever the performer, he could transform even a minor apology into a comic sketch sure to charm the recipient. 'My dear Kolle', he wrote in the spring of 1834,

> I am beyond measure distressed at your having had to wait for your coat... I entrusted it to our ex-man John Boston a long time since to take to the City, and a night or two since, he brought it back very coolly with an intimation that he had not had time to execute the commission – Never lend me another. I have got a severe cold which I suppose is a judgment upon me.

A self-depreciating apology, a droll defence, a plea for sympathy and a miniature character sketch all rolled into one brief note. It is easy to imagine that Dickens' energetic, obsessive immersion into any activity he chose to pursue – including returning a coat – may have made him a challenging companion at times. But his cheerful good nature and generosity surely outweighed his more difficult behaviour. Intensely convivial, Dickens continued to surround himself with close male friends even after he was married, finding them a source of both entertainment and emotional support.

Marriage was indeed imminent. By the time he was twenty-two, Dickens' social circumstances were improving and, with them, his chances for securing a wife. In 1834, he began reporting regularly for *The Morning Chronicle*, a Whig paper with a history of liberal journalism. Dickens was primarily a Parliamentary reporter, but he also wrote theatre reviews and travelled to report on election campaigns and public meetings. The position at *The Morning Chronicle*, a well-established paper competitive with *The Times of London*, provided Dickens an annual salary and thus his first steady income of five guineas per week. In December of that year, he moved out of his parents' house and into his own chambers at Furnivall's Inn. Proud of his hard-won success, the young man also smartened his dress, buying a new hat and blue velvet cloak that established a lifelong taste for brighter clothes that occasionally bordered on dandyism. Nevertheless, John Dickens' irritating financial difficulties continued. Constantly in debt, Dickens' father was arrested and placed in Sloman's sponging house in late November of 1834. This time, however, Dickens was no longer the helpless twelve-year-old who had been sent to the blacking factory. With his customary energy, Dickens took charge of the family problems, loaning his father money to get out of jail and finding cheaper lodgings for everyone near Bentinck Street. He temporarily moved his brother Frederick into his own chambers, exhausted his financial resources and even had to borrow some money from friends. Yet he did all this with a fair amount of compassion. Dickens was embarrassed, to be sure, but there is no evidence that his family's later money problems caused the same kind of trauma as their earlier financial crises. Dickens may have been too busy to care. He was working and writing furiously, publishing additional short stories between 1834 and 1835, and he had become romantically interested in a young woman named Catherine Hogarth, whom he had met in August of 1834.

Catherine was the daughter of George Hogarth, who had recently become the editor of *The Evening Chronicle*, a paper published by the owners of *The Morning Chronicle*. Impressed by Dickens' series, 'Street Sketches', which had been published in the fall and winter of 1834 in *The Morning Chronicle*, Hogarth asked him to write some short pieces for his paper. As payment for this additional work, the owners agreed to augment Dickens' reporting salary by two guineas per week, and he began a series entitled *Sketches of London*. Tremendously pleased with the young writer's gifts, the generous and hospitable George Hogarth invited Dickens to his house, where he soon became a regular guest. Dickens would join the large family for entertaining evenings of games, conversation and music. Catherine was the eldest child, just nineteen. In May of 1835, the two became engaged. Not even a full year later, on 2nd April 1836, they were married.

Like Maria Beadnell, Catherine was pretty, small, fair and tended towards plumpness. Unlike Maria, she was sweet, steady and predictable. No other suitors pursued her, and she demonstrated none of Maria's flirtatious fickleness. She was cheerful, warm and eager to please. Dickens devoted himself to her soon after they met. His early letters are tender and loving, addressed to 'My dearest Kate' or 'Katie', or, more simply, 'My Dear Girl'or 'My Love'. Later, there were silly nicknames: 'Mouse' and 'darling Pig'. They are often signed 'Believe me, My Love, Ever – Ever – Yours'. Dickens' affection for Catherine lacked the desperation of his earlier attachment to Maria. He wanted the stability, mutual affection and comfort of family life. Indeed, during their engagement, Dickens practiced all the domestic routines that he could while remaining respectable. For instance, he often invited Catherine over to breakfast with him, much as if they were already married and had awakened together as husband and wife. 'I hope to be awakened by *your* tapping at my door in the morning and I look forward on making my appearance in the sitting room, to find you heading my breakfast table,' he wrote to her in June of 1835. He asserted his rights before their marriage in other ways as well. When Catherine contracted a fever, he adamantly visited her despite the risk of infection. He often wrote and demanded that she meet him at particular places and times, insisting somewhat playfully on her punctuality.

For many years, Dickens welcomed the contrast in their personal styles, seeing Catherine's placid nature as a complement to his more frenzied spirit. He was all energy: hyperconscious of his professional responsibilities, ambitious and occasionally verging on manic. She was calm and agreeable. His upbringing had been somewhat erratic, and he was largely self-educated. She had been nurtured by warm and generous parents and had been instructed in subjects that respectable middle-class girls of the period were expected to learn: reading, languages, music, needlepoint. He was highly imaginative. She never manifested any creative aspirations. Dickens seemed to find these differences comforting, and his letters to his dear Kate suggest that she provided him with the calm and soothing support that he required to sustain his excessively busy professional life. During their engagement, he was travelling for the paper, writing reports and reviews and also composing his own sketches. Since his schedule allowed little time for courtship, he often wrote Catherine notes of apology for putting his work first. Whether it was his own nature or his fear of following in his father's footsteps, or both, Dickens was intensely disciplined and never missed deadlines.

Catherine proudly reported his accomplishments to her friends and family but also struggled to reconcile herself to the idea that Dickens was often less available than she would like. Sometimes she withdrew, hurt, and Dickens would inevitably scold her. In a letter from late May 1835, written almost immediately after their engagement and addressed coldly to 'My dear Catherine', he accuses her of capriciousness and indifference:

> The sudden and uncalled for coldness with which you treated me just before I left last night both surprised and deeply hurt me ... Depend upon it, whatever be the cause of your unkindness – whatever give rise to these wayward fancies – that what you do not take the trouble to conceal from a Lover's eyes, will be frequently acted before those of a husband.

Indeed, Dickens often managed what he called Catherine's 'coss' moods with a combination of teasing, guilt and bullying. The couple even sometimes referred to each other as 'Bully' and 'Meek'. Catherine usually accommodated him, finding it easier to give in than to resist. They remained mutually affectionate for years, but Dickens seems to have set the terms for the relationship.

Thus, at twenty-four, Dickens finally achieved the domestic security he had longed for. The marriage ultimately brought him not one but three wives of a sort. Catherine's sixteen-year-old sister Mary moved in with the couple for a month immediately after their honeymoon and stayed with them for extended periods thereafter. Her other sister, Georgina, joined the household six years later. Given the requirements of most large families during this period, it was not uncommon for single relations to move in with relatives, reducing the burden on parents and, in the case of women, providing another able body to help run the household. Mary was treated as a treasured companion rather than an imposition on the newlyweds. Even in the fairly small confines of their new lodgings at Furnivall's Inn, Dickens especially relished this amplification of his domestic arrangements.

Dickens' professional life also flourished at this time. In the autumn before his marriage, a young publisher named John Macrone approached him about purchasing the copyright to the Boz sketches and reprinting them in one volume. The enterprise was a bit of a gamble, but Macrone assumed all the financial risk. Looking toward the larger quarters and household furnishings he would need for his marriage, Dickens jumped at the chance. He thoroughly revised all the Boz sketches with the new format and audience in mind, pruning opening and closing paragraphs, deleting overly topical references and toning down any scenes that might be seen as vulgar. Macrone luckily managed to secure the popular artist George Cruikshank to provide the illustrations. Book illustrators at this time were often as readily recognised as authors, and sometimes they even dictated storylines. Cruikshank's fame far exceeded Dickens'. He had achieved widespread prominence in the 1820s with a series of cartoons that mercilessly lampooned George IV during the famous divorce trial of his wife, Queen Caroline. Despite Cruikshank's seniority and widespread reputation, Dickens proposed the title 'Sketches by Boz and Cuts by Cruikshank', placing the older and more famous man's name after his own. He then began to pester Cruikshank about the timeline for the plates, which were not always ready when he had hoped. Dickens was both obnoxious and admirably self-assured. Not even twenty-five, he already had the confidence of an important author who realised the necessity of establishing control over his work and his professional status. Macrone's edition of *Sketches by Boz* appeared on 8th February 1836 and sold quite successfully.

By the time *Sketches by Boz* came out in print, however, Dickens was already thinking about his next project. Two days after *Sketches* was published, William Hall, one half of the publishing firm Chapman and Hall, called on Dickens to invite him to write a monthly serial. Hall's original idea centred on a comical group of Cockney sportsmen and was designed primarily to showcase the cartoons of the popular artist Robert Seymour. Dickens had other ideas. With his customary boldness, he persuaded Hall to allow him to dictate the storyline, explaining that the illustrations should 'arise naturally' in response to his text rather than the other way around. They agreed that the work would be published in twenty instalments, each sold for just a shilling. Previously, most serial publications were devoted to reprints: the Bible, for instance, or *The Pilgrim's Progress* (1678). Dickens began writing on 18th February, spinning a picaresque tale of the exploits of The Pickwick Club, founded by the affable and sometimes absurdly innocent Mr Samuel Pickwick. Because it was originally conceived as a series of sketches, *Pickwick* is an eclectic mishmash of genres with a somewhat meandering action. (Dickens later noted in the preface to the complete edition that each serialised number was written to stand on its own.) Dickens attempts to pull the plot threads together at the end, but the book reads in many ways like a medley, interrupting the adventures of the Pickwickians for occasional short verse and various tales. *Pickwick* began serialisation in *The Library of Fiction* on 31st March, and the publishers printed 400 copies for the first run. At first, it looked as if the venture might be a total failure. Initial reviews disliked Dickens' satire of Parliament. Sales flatlined. Conflict emerged between Dickens and Robert Seymour, who felt that the tone of the writing – especially in the more sentimental and melodramatic sections – worked against his own comic style. In April, Dickens invited Seymour to his home, hoping to initiate a friendly and diplomatic dialogue about his problems with Seymour's sketch for 'The Stroller's Tale', one of the gothic short stories. The meeting was genial enough, but, two days later, Seymour unexpectedly committed suicide, shooting himself in the head at his summer house in Islington. The sad taint of the affair further jeopardised *Pickwick*'s ongoing publication. Chapman and Hall approached another artist, a wood engraver named Robert William Buss, but his lack of experience with etching failed to produce quality illustrations.

Then Chapman and Hall turned to another artist, Hablot Knight Browne. Shy and good-humoured, he got on with Dickens immediately. Browne's illustrations captured *Pickwick*'s tone perfectly. After four instalments, he began to sign his name 'Phiz' (after 'physiognomy') to complement Dickens' Boz. Their creative relationship lasted for twenty-three years, with Browne adapting his style to Dickens' as it evolved. The combination of Boz's writing and Phiz's illustrations was a hit. Published at a time when mass literacy levels were on the rise, the cheap instalments of *Pickwick* could be purchased and read by almost anyone, from servants – who could share them with friends or read them aloud to the less literate – to members of the aristocracy. The fourth number sold 14,000 copies, and, by the end of 1857, sales had reached 40,000. Mr Pickwick is a comic figure throughout much of the book, enduring one misfortune after another. Yet his good-natured benevolence endeared him to readers. Even more popular than Pickwick himself was his trusty servant, the pragmatic Sam Weller, known for his colloquial sayings, or 'Wellerisms', which were immediately collected and reprinted by other publishers. *Pickwick*-themed merchandise flooded the market in the form of hats, books, china figurines and other knick-knacks. (Today, these objects would function as marketing tie-ins that would benefit the author, but Dickens received no remuneration.) *Pickwick* also inspired a flurry of imitation and adaptation. The work was produced for the stage no fewer than five times before its publication had even concluded. It continued to sell well throughout the rest of the nineteenth century, and an estimated 1,600,000 copies had been sold in both England and America by 1878.

Dickens, of course, refused to rest. The year 1836 was extremely busy creatively, professionally and personally. At the same time that Dickens was writing *Pickwick*, he was also finally making a serious effort to write for the stage. He immersed himself in an adaptation of his own story 'The Great Winglebury Duel' (produced as *The Strange Gentleman* at the St James' Theatre on 29th September) as well as the libretto for an operetta entitled *The Village Coquettes* (produced on 22nd December). Both plays were moderately successful with the public, particularly *The Village Coquettes*, but neither was successful enough to lure Dickens into the world of the theatre for good. For all his flirtation with the stage, he earned more money and critical acclaim for his fiction. Toward the end of 1836, Dickens took his first important step toward becoming a full-time writer. He decided to resign his post as a reporter at *The Morning Chronicle* and to assume the position of chief editor of a new magazine, *Bentley's Miscellany*. Richard Bentley paid Dickens £20 per month for editing and twenty guineas for writing sixteen pages of original work for each issue. Between *Pickwick* sales and his new position, Dickens' yearly income was almost £800, far more than he had ever made before. (It is worth noting, however, that Chapman and Hall, who owned the copyright to *Pickwick*, turned a profit of at least £10,000.) The first issue of *Bentley's* appeared on 1st January 1837, one month before the debut of Dickens' second novel, *Oliver Twist*, and six days before the birth of Dickens' first child.

Indeed, 1837 witnessed both birth and death in the Dickens household. Charles Culliford Boz Dickens was born on 6th January 1837, exactly nine months after Dickens and Catherine were married. While Catherine was in labour, Dickens and Mary Hogarth, possibly evicted by Catherine's mother to get them out of the way, spent the day trying to find a table for her bedroom. The birth was straightforward and the infant healthy, but Catherine struggled to recover physically as well as emotionally. Because she was unable to nurse the baby and had to employ the services of a wet nurse, she worried that he would not love her. She burst into tears every time the infant wailed. Mary, who stayed the entire month after the birth to keep house for her fatigued sister and overcommitted brother-in-law, described Dickens as tenderly solicitous of Catherine during this time. Catherine recovered by the summer, but the condition (what we would now define as intense postpartum depression) plagued all her future pregnancies, gravely lessening her quality of her life for months at a time.

Dickens' joy in his first son was undermined by a wholly unexpected event: the death of Mary Hogarth at the young age of seventeen. On 7th May 1837, Dickens, Catherine and Mary had attended the theatre. Mary seemed perfectly healthy. Later that evening, while she was alone in her room, she collapsed to the floor with a cry before she could even undress. Despite the swift attendance of a physician, she died the next afternoon in Dickens' arms, the victim of a heart condition (aortic aneurism) that affected many in the Hogarth family. Devastated, it was the only time Dickens ever missed publication deadlines. He and Catherine had both adored the girl. Dickens saved a lock of her hair and wore a ring that he had removed from her finger – typical memorial gestures. But his grief achieved a pitch that was, if not disproportionate, at least a bit outlandish. He kept Mary's clothes, for instance, periodically viewing them for several years after her death. He told his friend Tom Beard in a letter that he was grateful that she had died in his arms, and that 'the very last words she whispered were of me' (17th May 1837). In his memory he idealised her, transforming her from an ordinary girl into an angel. 'I solemnly believe that so perfect a creature never breathed,' he continued to Beard. 'I knew her inmost heart, and her real worth and value. She had not a fault.' Some believe that the extremity of Dickens' passionate grief suggests that he was in love with his sister-in-law, but it may also be that the time he shared with Mary was simpler and less emotionally fraught than his work or marriage. Perhaps she symbolised the lost childhood innocence that Dickens so often yearned for in both his own life and his fiction, and which emerged with powerful feeling in *Oliver Twist*, written and serialised in *Bentley's* during this sad time of his life.

Oliver Twist departs rather abruptly and importantly from *Pickwick* both in form and theme. *Pickwick's* plot, a loose assortment of misadventures, lent itself to serial writing; Dickens conceived the whole of *Twist's* plot, by contrast, from the outset, imagining that it would one day be reprinted in volume form. It leaves the genial world of *Pickwick* for the desolate life of the London slums. The year 1837 was grim for England: the entire country faced a severe economic recession. Three years earlier, Parliament had passed the Poor Law Amendment Act, which centralised the country's system of poor relief and resulted in the establishment of more state-run workhouses. Even healthy paupers who had previously received assistance to augment their wages were now considered part of the 'idle poor' and forced into workhouses, where families were separated upon entry and children were forcibly removed from their mother's care after the age of seven. Living conditions were dehumanising, resembling harsh and unhygienic prisons. Inmates wore uniforms, were assigned physically demanding jobs with long hours and tried to survive on meagre food rations that consisted largely of bread.

Oliver Twist condemns the state's response to poverty and champions its child victims, making this novel Dickens' first sustained attempt to incorporate social reform into his fiction. Oliver's story reveals a world that brutalises women, children and the poor. Oliver is born then orphaned in a workhouse, and he eventually falls in with a gang of pickpockets run by a notorious

Jew, Fagin. (Dickens later apologised for his anti-Semitic portrayal of Fagin and attempted to counter it with his depiction of a benevolent Jew, Mr Riah, in *Our Mutual Friend*.) Dickens' portrait of Oliver's attempts to resist a criminal life – and the kindly individuals who take him in, assuming responsibility for his welfare when no one else will – critiques recent legislative efforts to regulate the downtrodden. He borrows theatrical tactics from the contemporary stage he so loved, such as stock villains and heroes as well as a melodramatic plot featuring virtue in jeopardy, to inspire both pity and political outrage in his readers.

Dickens conveys Oliver's plight with a special vehemence that points toward the presence of more personal preoccupations as well. From the time of his own unstable boyhood, Dickens was especially sensitive to acts of injustice perpetrated against children, and his extreme sympathy for Oliver may derive in part from his own memories of childhood vulnerability. His posthumous idealisation of Mary Hogarth may have also inflected his hyperbolic portrait of Rose Maylie, an angelic seventeen-year-old. Along with Cruikshank's vivid illustrations, Dickens' sentimental portrayal of Oliver and Rose helped to drive home his social criticism. Especially powerful are those moments where he suggests that even criminals are victimised by poverty. Bill Sikes' brutal murder of Nancy, for instance, transforms the prostitute from an object of condemnation to an object of sympathy, someone worthy of philanthropic attention rather than punishment. Dickens' brand of political radicalism did not necessarily include the details of social policy, but he held the government responsible for alleviating human distress even as he endorsed individual acts of human generosity. *Oliver Twist* illustrates the combination of sentiment and political critique that Dickens deploys in his future novels, and it was a smashing success, spawning numerous stage adaptations. It also inspired political debate. Even Queen Victoria, who had ascended the throne during its publication, tried to persuade the Prime Minister to read it.

Oliver Twist concluded its run in *Bentley's* in April of 1839. Dickens had already begun his next novel, however, in January of 1838, once again following an exhausting pattern of overlapping work that lasted throughout his career. *Nicholas Nickleby* (published by Chapman and Hall between April 1838 and October 1839) and *Oliver Twist* share a similar preoccupation with defending the underclass. *Nicholas Nickleby* focuses particularly on the cruelties of the school system for poor children. Such schools often operated like orphanages and workhouses, collecting unwanted children and subjecting them to harsh treatment. Dickens and Hablot Browne travelled to Yorkshire to visit an academy for poor boys, which confirmed Dickens' suspicions that the conditions were deplorable. *Nickleby* features as its eponymous hero a young schoolteacher who refuses to overlook his school's corruption and leaves his post, taking Smike, one of the most pathetic and helpless students, with him. For all the anger Dickens levels at the treatment of poor schoolchildren, the book also includes sustained comic interludes as Nicholas and Smike haplessly attempt to make a living. Dickens funnels his love of the stage into his affectionate portrait of the Crummels family's travelling theatre troupe (featuring the ageing 'Infant Phenomenon'), which becomes an eccentric but tender alternative family for Nicholas. *Nicholas Nickleby* never received the same critical interest as *Oliver Twist*, but its humour contributed to Dickens' growing reputation, and its first serial number outsold both *Pickwick* and *Oliver Twist*.

As if editing a journal and writing two novels were not enough, Dickens' family was growing as well. The first six years of his marriage produced no fewer than six pregnancies. Catherine miscarried twice, once not long after Mary's death (both she and Dickens believed the stress may have contributed to the loss) and again two years later, in 1840. She gave birth to the couple's second child on 6th March 1838, a daughter named Mary (called Mamie) after the aunt she would never know. Another daughter, Katherine (Katey) Elizabeth Macready, was born in October of 1839. Her name reflects the Dickenses' friendship with the actor William Charles (W. C.) Macready and exemplifies Charles and Catherine's habit of naming their children after prominent literary or cultural figures. (The first such figure, of course, was Dickens himself, who shows up not once but twice in the name of his first son, Charles Culliford Boz. One of their later children, Alfred D'Orsay Tennyson, was named after England's Poet Laureate.) Dickens was especially close to his daughters. Of all his children, Katey was the most like him: smart, funny and passionate. Dickens nicknamed her 'Lucifer Box' because her temper could be ignited as quickly as a tinder box. She and her father clashed later in life, particularly when Dickens disagreed with her choice of husband. Mamie, by contrast, remained her father's devoted helpmeet. She never married and lived with Dickens until his death.

On 31st January 1839, Dickens resigned his position as editor of *Bentley's Miscellany*. Tensions between Dickens and Richard Bentley had begun during the publication of *Oliver Twist* when Dickens somewhat presumptuously decided that the novel should count as one of the two novels that Bentley had already contracted him to write. Undoubtedly stressed by the mounting pressure of having committed to too many projects at once, Dickens saw no problem in demanding that his contract be renegotiated. Even though he was legally in the wrong, he was troubled by a justifiable feeling of having been ill-used with earlier contracts and felt convinced that he now deserved more flexibility. Annoyed, Bentley still attempted to accommodate him and eventually renegotiated the terms of the contract to include *Oliver Twist*. He made other concessions to Dickens as well, but Dickens characteristically had trouble letting the conflict go after having worked himself into a posture of outraged self-righteousness. His general grievances, moreover, had merit: his publishers were profiting far more than he was from his labour. Further disputes soured the relationship permanently. Dickens was now free to work on his own projects without the hassle of editorial work. He was barely twenty-seven years old.

The Inimitable
1839–46

After resigning his post at *Bentley's* in 1839, Dickens began a balancing act that would characterise the rest of his life. He juggled multiple overlapping writing projects, contract negotiations and the responsibility of supporting his household. Much to his dismay, he occasionally supported his extended relations as well. Now an established author, he was increasingly invited to speak publicly on the pressing social issues that he tackled in his fiction. With the financial resources that came from his writing, Dickens took a new house for his growing family on Doughty Street, now preserved as the Dickens Museum. It included a library that he could use as his own private study, and he stocked it with expensive editions of his favourite books. He also delighted in spending time with his young children and often chose to transport the entire family, including an entourage of servants, on his trips abroad. In an strenuous burst of productivity, Dickens not only wrote three new novels over the course of the five years that followed his departure from *Bentley's*, but also completed one of his best-known works: *A Christmas Carol*.

He began, however, with a journal. In July of 1839, Dickens pitched the idea of launching his own periodical, *Master Humphrey's Clock*, to Chapman and Hall. His journal would conform to the conventions of the time with one surprising exception: Dickens wanted to be its only contributor. Chapman and Hall agreed, and, for the first time in Dickens' life, the contract he signed met with his satisfaction, giving him both a weekly salary and a share in any future profits. At first, Dickens envisioned the journal as a miscellany, an assemblage of short sketches, essays and letters. As an organising conceit, he proposed that he would write the contents as if they had been discovered inside of Master Humphrey's grandfather clock. (Dickens would deploy the device of the unifying frame tale throughout his journalistic career.) *Master Humphrey's Clock* sold well at first, but even the resourceful Dickens struggled to sustain the diverse array of pieces that he had initially imagined. When sales began to drop, he decided to return to a story from the fourth number, 'The Old Curiosity Shop'. Featuring Little Nell and her loving but financially imprudent grandfather, the story soon consumed the entire journal. Dickens eliminated Master Humphrey and only returned to him at the very end, when he resurrected the character to announce that another novel would be forthcoming and that he was the great-uncle of Little Nell.

Although Dickens may have based his decision to expand the story on falling sales, the beautiful and virtuous Little Nell seized his imagination, and he deployed his considerable powers of sentiment to tell her story. Indeed, Dickens wrote the girl so sympathetically that even he second-guessed his original plan to kill the character at the novel's conclusion. Dickens had broached the topic of child death in his earlier fiction – the mournful portrayal of Smike's passing in *Nicholas Nickleby* was his most recent rendering – but it was Little Nell who crystallised Dickens' long-term preoccupation with delicately ethereal children whose tenuous hold on life imbues them with a special purity. Through their otherworldly innocence, these characters have the capacity to help adults achieve spiritual redemption. Nell's death was a stock trope (the motif of the angelic child was already in circulation in Anglo-American culture), but Dickens infused it with his trademark intensity, amplifying its emotional effect with his own metaphors and rhythms. His characteristic use of repetition becomes one of the hallmarks of Nell's death, as the doleful phrase 'She is dead' tolls dirge-like throughout the scene. The reading public responded to Nell's death with equal intensity. Her demise inspired a national outpouring of emotion. Grown men wept. Dickens had been calling himself 'The Inimitable' for years, and Little Nell's death showed that his writing indeed produced unique effects. Newspapers compared Dickens to Shakespeare, with Little Nell as a modern-day Cordelia. Legend has it that crowds gathered on the docks of New York to await the latest instalment, begging to know if Little Nell had survived. Given Dickens' extreme popularity in America, this scenario is probable. Ironically, he received no payments for the American editions of his work, which were pirated without permission from his publishers.

Dickens' closest source of professional support during this intensely creative time was his friend John Forster, who helped to broker the contract for *Master Humphrey's Clock*. Despite periodic disagreements, Forster would remain a lifelong friend, the co-executor of Dickens' will and also his first posthumous biographer. Indeed, much of what we now know of Dickens comes from Forster's account (it is worth noting, though, that as Dickens' friend, Forster tended to sanitise the less savoury aspects of Dickens' personal life). The two men had first met on Christmas Day in 1836 when they were both twenty-four. Forster belonged to Dickens' most recent set of male companions, a group of artists and writers associated with *Fraser's Magazine*. Like Dickens, Forster was imaginative, exuberant and cheerful. Like Dickens, he aspired beyond his origins (he was the son of a butcher and cattle dealer). The two men also shared a love of the theatre. When they first became acquainted, Forster had been writing on literature and theatre for several London papers, and he eventually reviewed a performance of Dickens' play, *The Village Coquettes*. He complained that the libretto was unworthy of Boz and gently poked fun at Dickens' dishevelled, post-performance appearance. Dickens laughed at his remarks. The two began to correspond, and soon they became close companions. Forster's business sense repeatedly saved Dickens from signing unfavourable contracts, and, by the 1840s, he began to act as an informal agent, often interceding directly with publishers. Dickens also frequently used Forster as a sounding board. When he conceived of *Master Humphrey's Clock*, for instance, he wrote a long letter describing the idea to Forster before he presented it to his publishers. Forster even read many of Dickens' manuscripts, offering liberal advice and sometimes making minor deletions. He later claimed credit for having persuaded Dickens to stick with his plan of writing Little Nell's death.

Just seven days after *The Old Curiosity Shop* concluded, Dickens began a novel radically different in theme in the pages of *Master Humphrey's Clock*. *Barnaby Rudge*, which ran from 13th February to 27th November 1841, was Dickens' first attempt at a historical novel. Since 1836, he had been planning to write a story that revolved around Lord Gordon's fomentation of riots opposing Catholicism in the 1780s, but various other projects and contract disputes had delayed it. The novel was an outlet for Dickens' long-standing interest in the Newgate prison and his opposition at that time to capital punishment, which had been strengthened by his visit to an execution the year before. His depiction of the slow-witted and normally gentle Barnaby Rudge shows how swiftly one can be seduced into joining a violent mob. Hoping to thrill readers with a dramatic historical setting, Dickens clearly revelled in imagining what it was like for rioters to break into and set the old Newgate prison aflame. But *Barnaby Rudge* sold poorly and remains the least liked of Dickens' novels. Even today, most readers find the historical setting burdensome and the plot less than engrossing. Although the flirtatious Dolly Varden became a popular Victorian heroine, inspiring bonnets and other fashions, the novel's most enduring character is a bird. Grip, Barnaby's talking pet raven, was named after Dickens' own bird. A pet lover in general – he adored dogs and owned a series of ravens – Grip was one of Dickens' favourite household animals. When the bird died, he had it stuffed and mounted and wrote comically grotesque letters to friends about mourning its passing. Grip had an unexpectedly long legacy. Edgar Allen Poe, who reviewed *Barnaby Rudge*, used Grip as the inspiration for his famous poem 'The Raven', written four years later.

Since Sir Walter Scott's novels had inspired Dickens to take on a historical novel, it was fitting that in the middle of writing *Barnaby Rudge*, he and Catherine took a summer trip to Scotland. On 25th June 1841, a huge dinner thrown in Dickens' honour in Edinburgh drove home the scale of his celebrity. Catherine's Scottish heritage only increased people's adoration of him, and the couple had a magnificent time touring the region. Dickens had very positive feelings about the trip, but the overwhelming reception also impressed upon him the necessity of producing fresh work to sate the appetite of his reading public. Dickens had begun to see Scott as emblematic of a novelist who had lost his creative energy, and he feared that he might share the same fate if he did not rest. By the time he had returned home and finished *Barnaby Rudge*, he was determined to take some time off.

Several factors contributed to Dickens' overall fatigue, the most alarming of which was an unexpected health problem. Dickens had developed an abnormal passageway (or fistula) in his anus that caused him great pain. In the autumn of 1841, he endured rectal surgery without anaesthesia. The operation left him bedridden while finishing the final instalments of *Barnaby Rudge*. Not surprisingly, he described this to his friends as a most harrowing experience, and the pain he suffered along with the difficulties that accompany recovery from such surgery left him physically drained. Emotionally, he also had to deal with the unexpected death of Catherine's brother, George, who was buried in Mary Hogarth's grave, a place Dickens had hoped to save for himself. Creatively, the close publication of his last two novels had worn him out. To refresh his spirits, he set his eye on travelling and selected America as his destination. Dickens felt sympathetic to American democracy, and, as a perpetual advocate for the downtrodden, he anticipated that America would offer an alternative model to England's entrenched class system. He also hoped to profit from the British appetite for books about their American counterparts and signed a contract with his publishers promising them an account of his travels.

Dickens' children posed the biggest challenge to the trip. In February of 1841, another son, Walter Savage Landor, had been born to the family, and Catherine did not want to leave the infant and her three other youngsters for such a long time. Yet taking Charley, Mamie, Katey and a baby on such an ambitious trip would hardly be practical. Despite Catherine's continued and strong opposition, Dickens continued to urge her to travel with him. Finally, he convinced her to leave the children with their close friend W. C. Macready and his wife, assuring her that his brother Frederick would also check on them regularly. Dickens then prepared for the voyage with his customary zeal, reading over twenty guidebooks and booking passage for the two of them on a steamship that departed on 3rd January 1842. A stormy fifteen-day journey across the Atlantic left both Charles and Catherine feeling seasick most of the time. Dickens, who complained about the dangers for weeks afterward, booked their return passage on a sailing ship.

Their arrival in Boston was considerably more felicitous than the journey itself. America welcomed Dickens warmly, eager to honour him with public dinners and balls (called 'Boz Balls'). He was treated as a celebrity and used the opportunity to wade into an international copyright debate, arguing publicly for better protection for authors. The pace of the trip was gruelling. In addition to the festivities in his name, Dickens also continued his practice of touring public institutions – hospitals, prisons, orphanages, asylums, factories – and even attended a session of Congress. He enjoyed the novelty of the trip at first. As a respite, however, it failed: Dickens had not counted on how much it would sap his strength. Always on display, frequently ill, homesick for his children, and taxed by the harsh winter weather, journeying through a strange country began to feel arduous. It also altered his romantic view of North American wilderness. He was awed by Niagara Falls, but the further Dickens travelled from major urban centres, the more edgy he felt. Catherine, less physically robust, was often similarly miserable but performed her wifely duties with dedication and grace, going out of her way to be sociable. Later, Dickens fondly commended her for her perseverance and she, in turn, remembered his kindness to her on the trip. After only one month in America, Dickens determined to stop making public appearances and swore (with moderate success) to complete the rest of the trip as a private tourist. Despite his disavowal of public life, Dickens continued to extend the threads of his social network, cementing his friendship with Washington Irving, with whom he was already in correspondence prior to the trip, and striking up friendly relations with some of America's other leading writers and public intellectuals.

Dickens' appreciation of this welcoming intellectual community, however, was severely undermined by his encounter with the American South and with slavery specifically, which he made an effort to witness first-hand in Richmond, Virginia. After he returned, he published his critique of the American institution in the account of his journey, *American Notes*, published in October 1842. Dickens approached slavery with the same reformist commitment that drove his depiction of English workhouses. He described the degradation of the housing, the dehumanisation of the slaves, and the general 'air of ruin and decay' that permeated the plantations. Often thought of as an essentially English novelist, Dickens' own view of himself as a reformer was global, or at least Anglo-American. He knew that his book on America would be read by the citizens of the very country he was writing about and felt that he could help American audiences to recognise the horrors of slavery with fresh eyes. In that sense, Dickens' portrayal of slavery in *American Notes* points toward the importance of transatlantic exchange to social reform in the nineteenth century. There were considerable tensions between America and Britain at this time over slavery, and Dickens' work participates in the larger debate that helped to shape social policy on both sides. Dickens incorporated further criticism of slavery into his next novel, *Martin Chuzzlewit*, which ran serially from January 1843 to July 1844. The novel chronicles young Martin Chuzzlewit's journey to America, which Dickens suggests is a country rife with speculators and shady deals. Dickens' portrayal of American slavery – its brutality, its immorality, and the vulgarity of its perpetrators – is one of the novel's primary vehicles for its main theme: the condemnation of human selfishness. *American Notes* is not always a flattering portrait, but Dickens' depiction of America in *Martin Chuzzlewit* is remarkably satirical, almost cynical. American readers responded to the novel's somewhat unexpected tonal sharpness with open hostility.

Martin Chuzzlewit was the last novel that Dickens organised around a picaresque journey, but, in his own life, travel became a major theme in the form of both short excursions and longer trips. In many respects, Dickens had always been a traveller. His unparalleled intimacy with London's streets, for instance, could not have been achieved without his wide-ranging walks, unusual for their speed and distance even in an era before mass transportation. It may be difficult to believe that Dickens had any excess energy to spare after writing for hours, but he chose to clear his head with physical activity and would walk about London or the countryside for hours at a time, sometimes covering as much as twenty or thirty miles and literally wearing out his companions. Dickens and the family also travelled frequently to the English countryside and would spend entire summers in Broadstairs, Kent. Abroad, Dickens was especially fond of France and Italy, where he repeated his practice of taking long walks. He spoke some French, and, after his first trip there in 1844, he returned to the Continent for extended periods when he felt depressed, was creatively blocked or wanted to avoid being in the public eye of his home country. Dickens took

Italian lessons with Catherine and travelled there with the entire family between July of 1844 and June of 1845. They stayed in Genoa, and Dickens and Catherine ultimately journeyed south alone to visit Pisa and Rome, where Dickens observed the rituals of Holy Week with some disdain. He published an account of these travels as *Pictures from Italy* (1846), capitalising again on the popularity of travel narratives. He also spent some of his time in Italy indulging his interest in mesmerism, and he hypnotised his friend Madame de la Rue on several occasions. While all this travelling helped Dickens to define his own sense of Englishness, it also gave him an important perspective on the eccentricities, successes and problems of his own country.

Dickens' increased fame brought new opportunities for him to address those problems and to exercise his reformist spirit. His novels' dedication to social reform often resulted in him being treated almost as a politician. Several boroughs asked him to run for Parliament, and, although he declined those offers, he rarely hesitated to turn down invitations to speak publicly about current affairs alongside politicians. For the speech Dickens delivered at the October 1843 opening of the Manchester Athenaeum, he shared the stage with MP Benjamin Disraeli twenty-five years before he became Prime Minister. To reach his audience of working-class adult students, Dickens delivered a blistering attack on ignorance and poverty, advocating that all social classes must work together to improve society. Dickens was often joined in his philanthropic efforts by Angela Burdett-Coutts, a young heiress who was one of the wealthiest women in England and whose family owned the bank where he kept an account. Burdett-Coutts shared Dickens' compassion for the poor, and he visited various institutions on her behalf to determine where she might best direct her charity. She provided the financial backing for more than one of Dickens' philanthropic projects.

Navigating his role as an ever more public figure was not the only complication in Dickens' life at this time. He also faced significant family demands. As usual, Dickens' parents continued to annoy him. Several years earlier, Dickens' father had racked up more debt, borrowing money from Chapman and Hall during the publication of *Oliver Twist*. In 1839, in an attempt to sort out his family's affairs and forestall any injury to his growing reputation, Dickens had finally installed them in a house in Devon, well away from his own life. It did not produce the desired effect. They complained about having been banished to country life, and Dickens' father persistently harassed his friends and publishers for loans, even targeting Burdett-Coutts. His brother Fred, following suit, was also in debt. More importantly, Dickens' immediate family increased his responsibilities. Dickens could be tenderly supportive and loved his young children passionately, but his time was occupied. By 1843, Catherine was raising four children under the age of six. To cope with the burden of so many young ones, the family invited Catherine's fifteen-year-old sister Georgina to stay with them as a companion, and she had moved in permanently by early 1843.

Women at this time were expected to aspire to motherhood, and there is no evidence that Catherine resented her role. Still, even with the help of Georgina and several servants, the physical and emotional strain was substantial, especially since Catherine had fewer opportunities to leave the house than her husband. Clever and cheerful, 'Aunt Georgy' shouldered considerable responsibility in the Dickens household despite her youth. Soon, the entire family depended on her. For the children, she was both playmate and teacher, keeping them occupied when their parents needed a rest and helping them learn to read. For Catherine, she facilitated domestic life on all fronts. She nursed her through the late stages of pregnancy and subsequent depressions and occasionally took on the role of hostess when Catherine was unwell. For Dickens, she became a walking companion, a ready participant in his amateur theatricals and even performed various secretarial duties. Like her sister Mary before her, Georgina's presence was welcomed rather than seen as intrusive.

These domestic arrangements also occasioned new expenses, and, unfortunately, *Martin Chuzzlewit*'s sales were not rising to Dickens' expectations. On top of receiving somewhat mixed reviews, it was published during a trade depression. Dickens hoped to alleviate the financial strain on his household with his new idea for a Christmas story. He envisioned it as an expensive volume with both colour and black and white illustrations by John Leech and began work on it in the midst of writing *Chuzzlewit*. In about six weeks, Dickens had finished composing *A Christmas Carol*. It was the first complete novel (or novella, given its short length) that he wrote without the formal constraints of the serial instalment, and it reveals him at his most confident and authoritative. The narrative builds without hesitation, never losing momentum. Dickens had always loved Christmas and had included it in his fiction before 1843, but *A Christmas Carol* represents a perfect fusion of his comic, fanciful side with his interest in the moral necessity for social reform. Dickens plots the story like a fairy tale – by now, everyone knows the story of the spirits who reveal scenes from Ebeneezer Scrooge's life to help him regain his generosity yet its savage condemnation of 'Ignorance and Want' attacks very real Victorian problems. Both Scrooge and the crippled boy Tiny Tim immediately became iconic figures: the former for his miserliness, the latter for his redemptive purity. Dickens' portrayal of Tiny Tim is one of his most effective uses of melodramatic sentiment. His crutch, his iron brace, his feeble voice: the very frailty of his body invites readers to shed tears. His physical presence testifies to the corrosive effects of poverty, but his own faith in God comfortingly confirms the presence of a larger moral order. Tiny Tim's 'God Bless Us Every One' is perhaps one of the most intense distillations of Dickens' Christian humanitarianism, which prioritises the potential for personal transformation and generosity in every individual over literal religious institutions. Dickens also emphasises the importance of the domestic sphere, contrasting the intense warmth of the

Cratchits' small home with the bitter cold of the streets. His suggestion that the family was the source of moral imagination and stability in a cruel urban world struck an instant chord with readers.

The book sold 6,000 copies almost immediately and went into multiple reprints. It did not, as some have suggested, invent Christmas. Christmas already existed as a one-day holiday complete with presents for children. Dickens' vision of how to celebrate it, however, crystallised those aspects of the Christmas holiday that Victorian culture in 1843 was poised to embrace: generosity, domestic harmony, festive entertainments and commercial exchange. With a new queen on the throne and a widespread rejection of evangelical Puritanism on the horizon, the country was ready for a grander celebration. Scrooge's complete transformation to besotted uncle and second father to Tiny Tim is excessive; by the end of the book, he is glutted with benevolent good cheer. *A Christmas Carol* derives its power precisely from this excess. Dickens' hyperbole proposed a new ethos for the holiday, and the aftershocks of *A Christmas Carol* reverberated throughout the rest of the nineteenth century. Christmas traditions sprang up in the wake of its publication: cards, crackers, carols, and the Christmas tree, courtesy of Prince Albert, who imported the tradition from Germany. Dickens' book was not the single catalyst for each of these developments, but it indelibly shaped the cultural terrain that allowed them to occur.

Unfortunately for Dickens, *A Christmas Carol* did not bring him the financial windfall for which he had hoped. It was immediately plagiarised and reprinted without Dickens' permission, and the successful copyright suit that he brought against the illegal publishers wound up costing him £700. The beautifully bound book was so expensive to produce that Dickens saw only a couple of hundred pounds from the first printing. As usual, he wound up feeling betrayed and disappointed by the business side of his work, and, not long afterwards, he packed the entire family off to France to nurse his wounds. Nevertheless, he was anything but soured on Christmas. At home, the holiday held great significance for him. His children and friends later recounted grand Christmas and Twelfth Night parties at which Dickens would dance and revel energetically throughout the night. As Dickens' family circle continued to expand with the birth of two more sons – Francis (Frank) Jeffrey was born a month after the publication of *A Christmas Carol* in January of 1844 and Alfred D'Orsay Tennyson in October of 1845 – the domestic celebrations only became merrier. Looking forward to Christmas with Dickens was anticipated by friends, family and readers alike. Despite the financial bungle of *A Christmas Carol*, Dickens followed it up with several more Christmas-themed books: *The Chimes* (1844), *The Cricket on the Hearth* (1845), *The Battle of Life* (1846) and *The Haunted Man and The Ghost's Bargain* (1848). Collectively called *The Christmas Books*, these five works ensured that Dickens' name would be permanently associated with the holiday.

Literary Heroics
1847–57

In the late 1840s and throughout the 1850s, Dickens was an extraordinarily prolific man. He moved his professional life in new and exciting directions, penned some of the longest and most influential novels of his career, continued to father children and led the social life of a true celebrity. With the founding of the weekly journal *Household Words* in 1850, Dickens assumed the role of editor-in-chief in addition to contributing sketches and articles, which meant that he was working as an editor, journalist and novelist in addition to corresponding faithfully with his many friends and acquaintances. The sheer volume of writing Dickens produced during this period is remarkable. With the busy social schedule he continued to maintain, one might think that he had no time for leisurely pursuits, yet he was characteristically restless and continued his lifelong habit of taking long walks through the countryside or city streets. His family obligations also increased. Four of Dickens' ten children were born in the five-year period leading up to March of 1852, when Catherine gave birth to their final child, Edward. Between 1847 and 1857, Dickens enjoyed enormous fame, financial success and domestic stability, confirming his status as a dominant force on the literary scene.

The 1840s produced some of the most famous English fiction of the nineteenth century. Dickens was publishing his works alongside Charlotte Brontë's *Jane Eyre* (1847), Emily Brontë's

Wuthering Heights (1847) and William Thackeray's *Vanity Fair* (1847–8). To this rich literary field, Dickens added *Dombey and Son*, which he began writing in Switzerland. It was serialised from October 1846 to April 1848 in direct competition with *Vanity Fair*, and it appears to have been planned more comprehensively than Dickens' previous novels. Dickens' notes to himself, the cover design and letters to Forster indicate that he followed a clear plan through to the end. He even retroactively outlined some of the instalments after their publication, possibly as a reminder to maintain continuity in the next number. The planning resulted in a noticeably tighter end result, and *Dombey and Son* is often labelled as the novel that marks Dickens' shift to a more serious and sober tone. As usual, he included a host of lovably eccentric characters, such as Captain Cuttle (oddly obsessed with sugar tongs) and Florence's irrepressible nurse, 'the Nipper' (prone to indignant, over-the-top outbursts). However, his increasingly complex portrayal of human emotions, especially those of women, lends this novel a new air of maturity, and the plot is distinguished by its smooth interweaving of domestic and business matters.

Dickens' scathing portrayal of the proud and materialistic Mr Dombey indicts the individual man as well as a broader culture that Dickens saw as selfish and unfeeling. Just as Dickens shows the railway destroying the countryside and old English neighbourhoods, bringing ruin alongside progress, he depicts the businessman's quest for commercial success as enriching but also threatening to devastate the family. Mr Dombey values his long-awaited son, for instance, primarily because he is the future heir to his firm, a prioritisation of business over domestic love that contributes to the little boy's pathetic early death in a scene as painful for Dickens to write as Little Nell's. Paul's sister Florence, however, quickly becomes the novel's affective centre. Because Mr Dombey views Florence as a useless commodity, the girl must find her way through the world with no loving relatives, relying on friendly nursemaids and sympathetic acquaintances.

In many respects, Florence's story is more poignant than those of Dickens' true orphans because she is effectively abandoned in the same house as a living, breathing father. Readers were gripped by Dickens' heart-wrenching portrayal of Florence's constant craving for the slightest bit of attention, let alone love, from her father. An unequivocal success, each instalment of *Dombey and* Son sold over 30,000 copies, more than six times the number of instalments sold of Thackeray's *Vanity Fair*.

Dickens followed *Dombey and Son* with one of his most famous works, *The Personal History of David Copperfield*. Published from May 1849 to November 1850, *David Copperfield* follows the plot of a conventional *Bildungsroman*, or coming-of-age story, signalled by its famous opening line, 'Whether I shall turn out to be the hero of my own life, or whether that station will be held by anybody else, these pages must show.' It is Dickens' most autobiographical novel. He began composing it not long after his effort at writing his own life story but found it easier to graft his memories onto a fictional story rather than to write a straight autobiography. Dickens strongly identified with David, and, as he observed to Forster on 10th July 1849, he thought of the work as 'a very complicated interweaving of truth and fiction'. By including autobiographical elements in the novel and bequeathing the scrap of 'true' autobiography to Forster, Dickens managed to tell a version of his story without having to face the same type of scrutiny that a non-fictional autobiography would have invited.

Some of *David Copperfield*'s scenes and characters clearly echo Dickens' own life: the description of young David working in a wine bottle warehouse is lifted almost verbatim from Dickens' description of the blacking factory; David's infatuation with Dora Spenlow is reminiscent of Dickens courting Maria Beadnell; and Mr Micawber's simultaneous accrual of debt and genteel aspirations parallels Dickens' own father's domestic mismanagement. Dickens also draws upon his own past fiction for inspiration, taking up characters and motifs that appeared in his earlier novels and revising them in new ways. For instance, Uriah Heep's false humility and loyalty – embodied in his slithering handshake – is a most unsettling intensification of the conniving traits displayed by James Carker in *Dombey and Son*. And characters like Betsey Trotwood, who battles Heep and stray donkeys on her lawn with equal zeal, illustrate Dickens' regular use of humour as both a source of entertainment and a challenge to the idea of respectability for its own sake. Like most of Dickens' orphan characters, once David's parents are both dead, he finds multiple surrogate families as he navigates his way through maturity, figuring out through trial and error how to choose a wife, preside over a household, make the right friends and succeed in business ventures. At the novel's conclusion, David has found happiness (like Dickens) as a writer, and the perpetually debt-ridden and child-producing Micawbers, along with the novel's fallen woman, head to Australia in search of new lives and success. Here, Dickens resorted to a technique many Victorian novelists often used to take care of their misfit characters: if they did not quite deserve death but could not be accommodated into a proper domestic vision, they were packed up and shipped overseas.

Dickens himself was involved in encouraging and helping downtrodden women to use the Australian colonies for their rehabilitation. A little over a year before the publication of *David Copperfield*, Dickens worked with Angela Burdett-Coutts to establish a home where former prostitutes could learn skills that would help them to lead improved lives once they arrived in Australia. For over ten years, Dickens managed the operations of the home, called Urania Cottage. Hardly a cottage, it was large enough to house thirteen destitute women in addition to two women working as superintendents. Dickens was involved down to the minutest details, going to prisons to interview and choose the girls who would live at the home, selecting the clothing they would wear once there and even picking the linens that would be used at the residence. He claimed a high success rate for the women who passed through Urania Cottage's doors and took great pride in the endeavour because it was a way he could take direct action to improve the lot of others. Dickens did not just write books encouraging people to be more fair-minded and compassionate; he put his time and money where his pen was by attempting to help when he could. There are many anecdotal accounts of Dickens giving money to struggling people he met in his travels or in the streets, but Urania Cottage is distinctive as a sustained and meaningful effort at institutionalising his charitable inclinations.

Alongside his demanding writing schedule and philanthropic work with Burdett-Coutts, Dickens maintained a full and growing home life. His letters to Catherine include amusing anecdotes about the children's foibles and games, and the couple's conjugal activities certainly do not appear to have suffered as a result of Dickens' busy career. In the midst of *Dombey and Son's* successful serialisation, Charles and Catherine welcomed another son into the family. After a particularly arduous labour, Sydney Smith Haldimand was born on 18th April 1847. For the next birth, Charles was adamant that Catherine receive chloroform, a drug that had only recently been used in childbirth, to ease her pain. On 15th January 1849, five months before the debut of *David Copperfield*, Henry Fielding Charles was born more easily. By the end of that year, Catherine was pregnant again. With eight children already – five under the age of ten – she was exhausted. Despite her regular battle with postpartum depression and Dickens' confiding to friends that he felt financially burdened by the constant birth of more children, he clearly continued to desire Catherine sexually and she clearly did not refuse him – an important reality to note given later developments in their relationship.

These years were also a particularly harrowing time of loss for the Dickens family. After a long battle with tuberculosis, Dickens' favourite sister Fanny died in September of 1848, and her calm self-possession in the face of death moved him deeply, prompting him to reflect upon his own mortality and that of his children. Fanny's crippled son Henry, who had inspired Dickens' rendering of Tiny Tim as well as the frail Paul Dombey, died in January of 1849. Then, in the spring of 1851, John Dickens died not long after undergoing painful surgery for the urinary and kidney ailments that had troubled him for decades. Although Dickens had regularly complained about his father's financial irresponsibility and generally referred to him as a bother or an embarrassment, he grieved deeply. As the years progressed, his memories of his father softened, and he was able to appreciate the good as well as the bad in the man. Just ten days after John Dickens passed away, Catherine and Charles underwent one of their saddest trials. In August of 1850, after giving birth to a daughter named Dora Annie, Catherine slipped into such intense and protracted postpartum difficulties that she and Charles decided she should spend some time convalescing in Malvern. Dora stayed in London, and on 14th April 1851, she died suddenly while Dickens was at a public dinner. The shock of her death stunned Dickens, who had been playing with her just before he left for the event. He also had to face the terrible task of breaking the news to Catherine, who was already in a fragile state. Dickens decided to send Forster to Malvern with a letter beseeching her to come home on account of Dora being 'very ill' so that he could disclose the news of the death in person. When he did, Catherine was devastated, falling prostrate with grief for several hours, but she did not suffer the complete breakdown he had feared. Despite the trauma of losing an infant, or maybe because of the closeness that results from enduring such family losses with a loving spouse, Catherine was pregnant again shortly after Dora's death. She gave birth to their final child, Edward Bulwer Lytton, on 13th March 1852. Their other children remarked upon the tender relationship their father shared with the baby of the family, who was nicknamed 'Plorn' and who saw an extra playful side of his father.

Through all these arrivals and partings, Dickens was also enjoying one of his biggest, and newest, commercial successes: *Household Words*. The first issue of *Household Words* boldly set as its mission 'to live in the Household affections, and to be numbered among the Household thoughts, of our readers'. In this 'Preliminary Word', Dickens articulated the ambitious hope that the weekly journal he founded on 30th March 1850 would become a beloved and integral part of domestic life. The title comes from William Shakespeare's *Henry V* (IV.iii.52), a source of inspiration of such significance to Dickens that he included the full quotation, Henry's reference to kings' names being 'Familiar in their mouths as Household Words', on every issue's cover. Each week, then, Dickens likened the journal's ubiquity to that of famous kings, continually linking the concerns of individual families to political, social and economic concerns.

Available on Wednesdays (a few days in advance of the Saturday publication date), *Household Words* reached the large readership for which Dickens had hoped. It became a venue for major novels of the day, such as Elizabeth Gaskell's *North and South* (1854–5) and Wilkie Collins' *The Dead Secret* (1857), and enabled Dickens to communicate with the reading public on a regular basis. Each issue only cost two pence so the middle classes could easily afford it, and many labourers could fit shared copies into their budgets. The journalistic venture was so successful that it enjoyed a twenty-year existence under Dickens' leadership, surviving a name change to *All the Year Round* in 1859, and it continued to appear even after Dickens' death with his eldest son Charles at the helm. Dickens used the periodical to entertain readers with sketches, articles, the occasional poem and serialised fiction; to advocate for important social reform, such as improved education and clean water systems; and to respond to current events with wit and amusement. Some contributors, such as Wilkie Collins and Henry Morley, sent in work regularly, while others had only a single piece published. Dickens wrote over a hundred articles himself, not counting collaborations or the Christmas issues. Indeed, *Household Words* was not a project over which Dickens exercised distant editorial control; rather, he was intimately involved at all levels, dominating the tone, content and production of the journal that bore his name as its 'conductor'.

In naming himself the 'conductor', Dickens called attention to the collaborative nature of *Household Words*, and the metaphor aptly brings to mind the different roles he filled. Like a railway conductor collecting fares, directing passengers and managing the flow of rapidly moving people and things, Dickens managed the dissemination of information. Like an orchestra conductor, Dickens brought together various talents to produce what he hoped would be a highly entertaining result. Especially fitting is the image of an instrument that conducts energy – a creative lightning rod, so to speak. In this role, Dickens was the catalyst for an array of creative energies with an incredibly far-reaching field. While the conductor metaphor is appropriate, it is also somewhat troublesome because it effaces the identities of so many contributors. One obviously cannot make beautiful music by conducting an empty orchestra pit, and Dickens' journal relied heavily upon the talent of many unnamed writers. In jettisoning bylines for most pieces, Dickens followed the convention of most journals and newspapers of the period. Writers were expected to relinquish their authorial identity in order to assume the voice of the paper, and sometimes Dickens revised pieces so heavily that it would not necessarily have been more accurate to retain the original writer's name as the sole author. Some writers complained that Dickens' practices were exploitative. Others noted, by contrast, that Dickens paid contributors well and that many aspiring writers were honoured to have their pieces personally selected by and sometimes published alongside the work of a writer as illustrious as Dickens.

The annual Christmas number of the journal became an eagerly anticipated holiday event. After the enormously popular

Christmas Books, the special issues were Dickens' way of continuing his participation in the nation's December celebrations. He saw this as an enjoyable yet serious responsibility and felt the pressure of making sure he delivered a good Christmas number even when his other writing projects kept him occupied. Sometimes Dickens worked with just Wilkie Collins on these stories, but more often they contained pieces written by several authors, with as many as nine different writers contributing to a single number. Dickens would think up an idea for a framing structure and then use the contributors' stories to fill in the rest. *A Round of Stories by the Christmas Fire* (1852) has a very basic frame: storytellers are sharing tales as they sit around a fire. Later, though, the structures of the numbers were increasingly elaborate. In *The Wreck of the Golden Mary* (1856), the frame tale (penned by both Dickens and Collins) describes a shipwreck, and the middle is full of stories that the passengers tell each other to pass the time in lifeboats as they await rescue. *Somebody's Luggage* (1862) clearly revels in the playfulness of its frame, which tells of a waiter discovering various manuscripts stuffed into a set of abandoned luggage. The middle stories are appropriately named for the locations of their discovery – 'His Boots', 'His Writing Desk', 'His Umbrella' and so forth – which invites the reader to visualise how they fit together physically and metaphorically. The contributors did not discuss how their stories would complement each other or how they would respond to Dickens' directive. Still, startlingly coherent thematic threads or motifs appear with some frequency to link the stories together. Despite the sometimes uneven quality of the stories, Dickens' Christmas numbers were popular texts that inspired other journals and publishers to produce countless imitations.

Reviewing hundreds of manuscripts annually, Dickens had to have help managing the journal. For that, he relied on his sub-editor W. H. (William Henry) Wills. Wills kept careful track of how much each contributor was paid, and it is thanks to his meticulous record keeping in the journal's 'Office Book' that we know with certainty who wrote each published piece. He was indispensable to *Household Words*, yet his constancy is an often overlooked element of the journal's success. At a time when changes in periodical staffing were common, Wills, who held a share of the profits, was a consistent and professional sub-editor over an impressive span of nineteen years. A consummate copy editor and fact-checker, Wills also handled the logistics of printing and distribution, oversaw the day-to-day running of the office (especially when Dickens was away) and managed correspondence with all of the contributors. He even regularly wrote articles himself. Given the long-lasting nature of this partnership, the skirmishes between Wills and Dickens were fairly minor. They sometimes differed over how much contributors should be paid, and there were editorial tugs-of-war over changes to Dickens' own work, or work Dickens had himself edited that Wills then re-edited. This was a close relationship that Dickens came to rely on personally as well as professionally, and while Wills' poor health forced him to leave his post in 1868, the two men remained friends.

With Wills' assistance at the helm of *Household Words*, Dickens was able to continue his novel writing as well. It is astonishing to think of Dickens fulfilling his editorial duties and producing Christmas numbers at the same time that he was writing the massive *Bleak House*, which was serialised from March 1852 to September 1853. Considered by many to be Dickens' masterpiece, *Bleak House* is often regarded as the quintessential Victorian novel, with its huge cast, its multiple plot threads and its famously powerful depiction of the mid-nineteenth-century urban experience from the perspective of both the very poor and the very wealthy. Indeed, it begins with just one word: 'London'. The city and its associations are so vast that its name fulfils the functions of all a sentence's parts of speech at once. In this and other ways, *Bleak House* was an important literary experiment for Dickens. Throughout the novel, he plays with different forms of narration, telling some chapters from a third-person point of view and abruptly shifting into a first-person point of view in others. He also experiments with genre. With the character of Mr Bucket, a professional police inspector investigating a murder, *Bleak House* becomes an important forerunner to the detective novel.

Even with these formal innovations, Dickens revisits many of his favourite themes and motifs, taking up scenarios and characters from his earlier novels with increased sophistication. For instance, *Bleak House* indicts the modern legal system – particularly the court of Chancery – with the same vehemence that Dickens levelled at workhouses earlier in his career. And, like so many of Dickens' other protagonists, *Bleak House*'s Esther Summerson is a sympathetic orphan who finds herself at the mercy of well-meaning and powerful members of the higher classes. Much of the novel revolves around the mystery of her parentage and the legacy of a fallen woman's choices. Two of her friends, Richard and Ada, are wards of the court who follow their infamous case, Jarndyce and Jarndyce, through Chancery and are subjected to the whims of a legal system that makes no sense. Jo, a young crossing sweeper, is another child whose poignant death inspires rage at social apathy and an unforgiving urban environment. In the midst of these familiar characters, Dickens makes room, as always, for the grotesque and the comic. *Bleak House* includes one of the most famous literary depictions of spontaneous combustion ever written and is replete with figures like Mrs Bagnet, memorable for saving the day with greens, an ever-present umbrella and a most reassuring maternal strength. The novel sold well but received mixed reviews, since some readers were troubled by the force of Dickens' attack on established English social institutions. To recover from the demands of finishing it, Dickens visited Italy with Wilkie Collins and the painter Augustus Egg for a few months at the end of 1853, and he threw a celebratory party in Boulogne on 22nd August.

By 1854, sales of *Household Words* had begun to lag, and profits were dropping. For his next novel, Dickens decided to try to boost circulation by returning to the intensive weekly serial format he had abandoned after *Barnaby Rudge*. He began *Hard Times* on 1st April and concluded it on 12th August 1854 in twenty instalments. The tactic worked, and sales of the journal soared. But writing weekly rather than monthly instalments was too draining for Dickens to continue on a regular basis, and *Hard Times* is one of Dickens' shorter novels. Its brevity, however, does not lessen the intensity of its message. While in *Bleak House*, Dickens was concerned about the dirt and disease of London's streets, in *Hard Times* he shifted his focus to Coketown (a northern industrial city much like Manchester) and kept it there, making the novel the only one that occurs entirely outside of London for the duration of its pages. The novel is concerned with the prolonged oppression of the imagination in favour of an inflexible utilitarian educational system focused on 'facts' (one of the teachers is tellingly named Mr McChoakumchild). An excessive focus on facts and practicalities without consideration of unpredictable human factors such as emotion and curiosity results in a world of loveless marriages, needless suffering and stifled souls. The times in this novel are hard indeed, and its ending is unusually grim for Dickens.

In an attempt to stave off exhaustion from the gruelling pace of *Hard Times,* Dickens completed it in Boulogne, a city he often found to be restful and congenial to his creative labours. The next summer, the entire Dickens family travelled back to the Continent, ultimately settling in Paris from October 1855 to April 1856. Dickens made periodic trips back to England for business, and, during one such trip in February of 1856, he finalised the purchase of a new house: Gad's Hill, outside Rochester. Dickens had seen the house as a boy, and it retained a special place in his memory, symbolising prosperity and success. Gad's Hill ultimately became Dickens' permanent home, but, at this point in his life, he remained in Paris, where he began writing *Little Dorrit*. Inspired by Dickens' own change of scenery, the novel begins with a satirical portrait of a group of provincial English tourists in France. Yet instead of exploring the freedom or pleasures of international travel, the opening chapter zeroes in on the Marseilles prison looming in the sun. Prison is *Little Dorrit's* dominant metaphor. It focuses particularly on the long dark shadow cast by England's Marshalsea, where Dickens' own father had been incarcerated so many years ago. The story of a young girl born within the walls of the Marshalsea while her imprisoned father awaits relief from his debt, *Little Dorrit* is preoccupied not only with the institutional manifestations of prison, but also with its psychology, portraying a world where human beings deliberately incarcerate themselves within homes, marriages, jobs and habits. Repression in this novel is far more generalised and pervasive than it is even in *Hard Times*. *Little Dorrit's* Circumlocution Office, run by government servants trained in the art of 'How NOT to do it', is a sweeping metaphor for the all-encompassing presence of bureaucratic institutions that trap human beings in meaningless routines of endless, agonising repetition. Published from December 1855 to June 1857, the novel sold well, as most of Dickens' fiction did at that point in his career. But its complex plot and somewhat ambivalent conclusion did not inspire the same kind of public fervour as some of his previous work.

In the midst of writing *Little Dorrit*, Dickens turned to a completely different genre and indulged his love of the theatre by collaborating with Wilkie Collins on a play, *The Frozen Deep*, in late 1856. Dickens even acted in the play, performing the role of Richard Wardour, who is shipwrecked during an Arctic expedition only to find that the man who is nearly freezing to death alongside him is his rival in love. To great melodramatic effect, Dickens portrayed Wardour's choice to rescue rather than murder the fiancé of his beloved at the cost of his own life. Dickens and Collins produced this drama at Tavistock House, into which the family had moved in November of 1851, and the January 1857 performances were well received. In the summer, Dickens decided that additional performances would be an excellent way to raise money for the widowed family of his close friend Douglass Jerrold, who had died suddenly on 8th June. On 4th July, as they prepared for benefit shows at the Gallery of Illustration, the original amateur cast, which included Charles, Georgina, Mamie and Katey Dickens, performed the play privately for Queen Victoria, who was said to have enjoyed it. As Dickens began to plan events at the large Free Trade Hall in Manchester, he decided to use professional actresses for the endeavour. The legacy of Jerrold's death and the continued production of *The Frozen Deep* would lead directly to titanic changes for the entire Dickens family and to one of the greatest loves of Dickens' later life.

Partings
1857–70

From the summer of 1857 to the summer of 1858, Charles Dickens' life changed radically and dramatically. His choices during this period plunged the entire family into uncertainty and moved him away from a life of domestic stability to one of domestic chaos. Dickens started behaving in extraordinary ways: ending long-standing friendships, breaking with publishers, sleeping at his office for a time, pushing his eldest child away and publishing a most embarrassing piece of writing. What could inspire such behaviour in a man who had never been predictable but who had lived his life with a marked concern for propriety? Infatuation. Dickens decided he must end his marriage with Catherine and maintain what he hoped would be a secret relationship with a young actress named Ellen Ternan. The affair caused a scandal, and the relationship is one of the most hotly debated aspects of Dickens' late life.

Dickens met Ternan in the summer of 1857 when he was looking for professional actresses to take over the parts performed by his daughters and Georgina Hogarth in *The Frozen Deep*. With Mrs Ternan at the helm and sisters Maria, Fanny and Ellen working regularly on the stage, the Ternans were an established acting family. Fanny was the most talented actress, and Ellen, who went by the name Nelly, was the most stunning beauty. At the age of eighteen, her blue eyes, blonde hair and pleasant figure were known to turn heads, and her intelligence and quickness made her all the more alluring. As Fanny was busy with other work, the three remaining Ternans took parts for the Manchester benefit performance of *The Frozen Deep*. Over the course of their rehearsals and performances, Dickens became obsessed with Nelly, and the two began a long and intimate relationship. After the shows, Dickens struggled to concentrate on anything but her, changing his lifestyle so that they could spend as much time together as possible. What he saw in Nelly became the gauge by which he measured his wife, and things about Catherine that he had previously found bothersome now became completely unacceptable.

Just a few months after meeting Nelly for the first time, Dickens made the unilateral decision to separate himself physically from his wife. Without warning, he ordered a servant to construct a partition in their bedroom at home that would divide their private spaces. Dickens had the partition covered with bookcases, and his dressing room became his bedroom. Their shared bedroom was now Catherine's alone. Catherine had no input into the arrangement. Of course, this hurtful act distressed her, but she did not use it as a reason to leave the house. While Charles clearly was not interested in rehabilitating the marriage – indeed, he seemed bent on destroying the good feeling that remained – Catherine refused to be the one to make the final break. An event in the spring of 1858, however, hastened their ultimate separation. A jeweller sent a trinket, which some reports suggest was a bracelet, intended for Nelly to Catherine at Tavistock House. While Dickens regularly sent gifts to those who participated in his theatrical productions, Catherine felt that this particular gesture crossed a line. Shortly thereafter, Dickens insisted that she actually pay a visit to the Ternans, apparently to demonstrate that there was nothing inappropriate in the relations between the two families. In one of Katey's later accounts, she claimed that when she found her mother weeping over the prospect of the visit, she implored her to refuse, but Catherine again assented to Charles' wishes and went on what must have been a most awkward social call.

After this incident, the Hogarths urged their daughter even more strongly to pursue a separation, and the parties representing Charles and Catherine finally came to an agreement on terms so as to avoid legal proceedings. Catherine would receive £600 per year and live with her eldest son, while the rest of the children would remain with their father and Georgina Hogarth, who allied herself with Dickens over her own sister. Although technically the other children would be permitted to visit their mother, family correspondence and the children's own statements in later years make it clear that Dickens strongly discouraged them from seeing Catherine and forced them to choose his side in the dispute. The couple never spoke face to face again, almost never corresponded in writing and saw each other only once when they happened accidentally to attend the same theatre performance.

The split, and especially Dickens' manner of handling it, surprised many because he and Catherine were not known for being an acrimonious couple. Dickens sometimes complained about Catherine's depression and lack of energy, but he also expressed sympathy and love for her throughout their marriage. Many of Dickens' letters and reports from his friends, however, show that he increasingly represented himself as the victim of a dull, physically weak and intellectually slow spouse. Rather than finding a vivacious companion who could match him point for point in his wit, or mile for mile in his walks, Dickens began to suggest that he had spent over twenty years living with a woman whose goal was to drain rather than to inspire his creative energy. Of course, his own letters contradict this very story, and many of his friends and acquaintances did not fall for the new tale of prolonged marital suffering since they had witnessed the couple's domestic accord first-hand. It is almost as if Dickens threw himself into creating such an awful story of their union because he knew he was writing against himself, to negate his own earlier assertions of domestic happiness. This is not to suggest that there were no problems in the marriage, only to note that this is an area of Dickens' life where his actions and words must be examined with extra care.

Just as Dickens manipulated the way in which the story of his work at the blacking factory was told (or not told), he also continually created a narrative that would make him look like less of a villain in his separation from his wife. He was livid when he heard that rumours of his having an extramarital affair were circulating. Dickens believed that Catherine's mother and sister were spreading the gossip, and, even worse, he blamed them for speculation that the woman with whom he was consorting was his sister-in-law Georgina. The scandal was as much about *who* Dickens was denying having an affair with as it was about having an affair at all. It was only moderately better for people to assume that a young actress (rather than Georgina) was the object of Dickens' affection because actresses, who put themselves on display for pay, were often considered sexually suspect even late into the nineteenth century. For this reason, Dickens was outraged when he heard that Thackeray had stated at the Garrick Club that Dickens was committing adultery with an actress. Thackeray claimed that his comment was actually made in defence of Dickens because identifying the lover as an actress deflected accusations about Georgina. Nonetheless, Dickens listed Thackeray among his betrayers. Thackeray made a point of visiting and maintaining friendly relations with Catherine, and the men were not on speaking terms again until 1862, when Thackeray made the first moves to restore civility.

Given that Georgina lived in the Dickens household and chose to remain with Charles at the cost of separation from her entire family, speculation about the nature of their relationship seems inevitable. Some have suggested that Georgina was in love with him, which her friend Anne Thackeray thought to be true. Once the Dickenses separated, it was considered extremely unusual for Catherine's sister to remain in the home. Having an affair with his wife's sister would be tantamount to Dickens committing incest, and some rumours went so far as to suggest that

Georgina had bourne some of Dickens' children. Their reaction to this gossip was quite radical. In an act that was far more shocking than the rumours themselves, Georgina agreed to undergo a gynaecological exam to verify her virginity. Such an exam would have been not only personally insulting, but also an affront to the notions of modesty, propriety and virtue that defined respectable middle-class femininity. That Georgina consented to it suggests that she was willing to prioritise Dickens' reputation over her own, subjecting herself to embarrassment on his behalf and calling even more attention to her curious position in Dickens' household.

Dickens' hyperbolically sensitive and disproportionate reaction to any public criticism of his behaviour led him to further bizarre public displays. On 7th June 1858, he published a statement called 'Personal' in *The Times of London* that was later reprinted in *Household Words* and *The New York Times,* ensuring rather than decreasing talk about the scandal on both sides of the Atlantic. Dickens assumed that his entire reading public had been gossiping about his marriage when, in actual fact, many of them had not even heard about the affair until Dickens himself publicised it. In the statement, Dickens claimed that he had been the subject of 'misrepresentations', that his 'domestic trouble' was resolved and that 'its details have now but to be forgotten by those concerned in it'. He spoke for himself and for Catherine as he portrayed their split as amicable and absolved himself of guilt; indeed, he made the Hogarth family's endorsement of the statement a condition of the final separation settlement. Dickens' publishers, Bradbury and Evans, refused to honour his request that they publish the piece in *Punch* because such a private matter was completely out of place in a humorous journal. Dickens viewed their decision as a betrayal, broke with them and formed a new weekly journal called *All the Year Round*. Upon winning a Chancery suit over the rights to the name *Household Words*, he ceased its publication by folding it into *All the Year Round*.

The scandal did not end with the 'Personal' statement. On 25th May 1858, Dickens presented Arthur Smith, the manager of the benefit tour of *The Frozen Deep*, with a vitriolic letter in which he described what he considered to be Catherine's major flaws. In this especially nasty attack, Dickens accused her of having a 'mental disorder' and being an unfit mother who had 'thrown all the children on someone else'. That someone else was Georgina, whom Dickens credited with keeping the marriage together for so many years. When Dickens gave Smith the letter, his written instructions specified that Smith could show the letter to 'anyone who wishes to do me right, or to anyone who may have been misled into doing me wrong'. On 16th August 1858, it appeared in *The New York Tribune*, and English periodicals reprinted it shortly thereafter. Readers were shocked: both the private nature of the accusations and Dickens' caustic tone were wildly inappropriate for a public forum. Immediately after the letter's publication, Dickens claimed he never intended for it to be shared. He went so far as to refer to it as 'The Violated Letter' even though he never specifically blamed Smith for sharing it. Given that Dickens wrote the letter at the height of his anger about the rumours he believed the Hogarths to be spreading about a possible affair with Georgina, and given how long Smith waited to publish the letter, it is certainly possible that Dickens was caught off guard when he saw it in print in mid-August. Nevertheless, it is hard to believe that in the midst of a separation Dickens felt to be so public, he would have given a written statement to a person whose responsibility it was to manage his public appearances – with guidelines for the sharing of that statement no less – and expected it to remain uncirculated.

One of the most remarkable things about Dickens' actions during the dissolution of his marriage is that his behaviour makes little sense. His actions do not seem commensurate with those of a benevolent, charitable man concerned with the integrity of the family. For him to be the authoritarian wielder of patriarchal power is jarring when one considers how force-fully he derides such figures in his fiction. It is disconcerting for the champion of orphans to separate his children, the youngest only six years old, from their mother. At the same time, Dickens had a history of being a micromanager, even a bully (as Catherine's old nickname for him makes perfectly clear), when it came to managing both his periodicals and his home. He also had a penchant for drawing lines in the sand when he felt people needed to take a stand alongside or against his interests. Perhaps this episode from his life shows Dickens at his most human in that he engages in distasteful, and at times detestable, behaviours that disillusion those who would wish for him to remain a gilded celebrity icon — an image Dickens himself put enormous effort into maintaining.

Most of what we know about Dickens and Ellen Ternan comes from decoding references to Ternan in Dickens' letters. Unless new letters surface, some questions about their liaison will never be answered, but the ongoing work of scholars continues to reveal more details about Ellen Ternan herself, her relationship with Dickens and the lengths to which he went to disguise it. After the very successful Manchester performance of *The Frozen Deep*, which concluded its run with an extra show on 24th August 1857, there was no obvious reason for Dickens to maintain contact with the Ternans. They went to Doncaster for work in other theatricals, and he returned to Gad's Hill, where he immediately commenced writing to his friends about his restlessness. He felt stifled at home and craved release from an environment he found unbearable. To cure this angst, in mid-September, when he knew the Ternans would be in Doncaster, he proposed that he and Wilkie Collins take a trip there for a 'walking tour'. The remedy worked, and Dickens and Collins fictionalised their outing as *The Lazy Tour of Two Idle Apprentices* (1857), which features a character named Francis Goodchild obsessing about a golden-haired 'Angel' with whom he wishes he could spend eternity. Dickens did not succeed in guaranteeing an eternity with Ternan during the trip, but he was observed watching her perform in front of a raucous crowd. It is likely that she accompanied him to the famous Doncaster races, and he remained infatuated.

In October, Dickens wrote to John Buckstone, the manager of The Haymarket where Ternan was working, asking him to give Dickens warning of where Nelly would be working in the future even before informing Nelly herself. Something in their interactions had clearly led Dickens to feel comfortable assuming such a privileged and controlling role. He also recorded a payment to Buckstone that was likely meant for Nelly. But only knowing where she would be left Dickens miserable as he was slogging through the pending separation from Catherine. In March of 1858, Dickens wrote to Collins, 'The Doncaster unhappiness remains so strong upon me that I can't write, and (waking!) can't rest, one minute. I have never known a moment's peace or content since the last night of *The Frozen Deep*. I do suppose that there never was a man so seized and rended by one Spirit.' Even when writing privately to a close friend, Dickens used three different codes for Ternan, mindful of the consequences of public exposure even as he was distracted by his own anguish.

Dickens did not have to remain in such pain for long. By the end of 1859, Ellen Ternan had stopped acting entirely, and the two began to settle into a life of travel and secrecy. Even though Dickens did not feel comfortable living openly with Ternan as his mistress, he seemed satisfied with having found a confidante and companion. That Nelly was financially secure enough to stop working suggests Dickens' monetary support, and he probably bought her a house. Someone purchased No 2 Houghton Place on Ampthill Square for Fanny and Maria Ternan, and they transferred the lease to Ellen a year later when she came of age. While no paper trail names Dickens, there is no evidence to suggest that the family had another wealthy benefactor. Some records from the account that Dickens kept at Coutts Bank reveal expenditures on Nelly and her family (as well as some mysterious expenditures that may well have been for Nelly), which not only suggests the level of his commitment to her, but also confirms the long duration of the relationship. When Fanny Ternan published novels anonymously in *All the Year Round* in the 1860s, her payments were issued from the Coutts account instead of the journal's, presumably to keep her name hidden.

At the same time as Dickens was hoping to keep his affair with Ternan far away from the public eye, he began to cultivate a hyper-public existence. In the spring and summer of 1858, just as the separation was being finalised and Dickens was desperately trying to quell the rumours about Georgina and Nelly, he also gave his first public readings for profit. In December of 1853, Dickens had performed his very first reading for a benefit event in Birmingham. Reading from *A Christmas Carol* and *The Cricket on the Hearth*, he used the benefit as a way to test reactions to an author reading publicly from his own work, a new idea at this point in literary history. Forster and others had expressed concern that the for-profit performances would seem mercenary and might degrade Dickens' reputation as a novelist, but they were enormously successful. The performances regularly sold out, received rave reviews and were very profitable. He actually earned more from the readings than he ever did from sales of books. A reading desk of his own design and a book shared the stage with Dickens, and audiences were fascinated at how his voice and facial expressions enabled him to embody his own characters. He threw himself into these performances so completely that they left him physically wracked, and he sometimes had to lie down for half an hour afterwards in order to recuperate. Still, Dickens delighted in the shows – the close contact with his readers as well as his characters – and maintained a rigorous touring schedule for the rest of his life.

It seems contradictory for Dickens to be complaining about overexposure regarding his personal life while he made a spectacle of himself on stage, but Dickens' actions suggest that he could not escape embodying contradiction. There was simply no way to reconcile his desire for public love and approval with personal behaviour that he knew many would repudiate. He might, for instance, have been able to predict that Angela Burdett-Coutts, with whom he worked so hard to establish and superintend Urania Cottage, would be displeased with the way he dissolved his marriage and carried on with a young, unmarried actress. Indeed, after a visit from Catherine and some of the younger children, Burdett-Coutts urged Dickens to seek a reconciliation. As with his publishers Bradbury and Evans, Dickens saw no room for disagreement. Once it was clear to him that Burdett-Coutts would not unequivocally endorse his actions, he decided to end not only their friendship, but also their professional partnership. In deciding to cease his involvement with Urania Cottage, Dickens chose to prioritise his feelings about his personal life over his concern with helping fallen women, and it does not appear to be a decision over which he anguished. The ease with which he walked away from such a long-standing philanthropic project, and one that was specifically focused on helping young women who made bad decisions about men, reveals much about how Dickens' frame of mind had changed at this point in his life. While it is always risky to guess at what a man as varied and complex as Dickens was thinking, it is certainly possible that his affair with Ternan made continuing work at Urania Cottage hypocritical, even if Dickens would never have admitted it.

Dickens could not bring himself to break publicly with domestic convention even though precedents for such breaks existed. Despite the powerful cultural and religious expectations structuring Victorian marriage and family life, many people found ways to negotiate their way out of unhappy relationships, as some of Dickens' own friends demonstrated. He associated with George Eliot (Marian Evans) and George Henry Lewes, who lived together unmarried because Lewes was unable to divorce his wife. Eliot and Lewes were excluded from some polite circles, but the scandal of living out of wedlock did not substantially diminish Eliot's popularity as a novelist. Wilkie Collins openly maintained two households, and Dickens did not hesitate to visit with him and his mistress or to continue collaborating very publicly with Collins on writing projects. Socializing with Collins and other young male friends provided Dickens with a community of younger admirers who did not chastise him for spending time with Nelly rather than remaining with Catherine. Dickens had tried to convince Catherine to agree to a private arrangement where they would maintain the appearance of a marriage while living in separate quarters or households, splitting their time between Tavistock House and Gad's Hill. But Catherine firmly rejected such ideas. Once they were separated, Dickens did everything in his power to avoid exposing his current lifestyle.

Dickens' wish to keep Ternan's presence in his life a secret was fulfilled for a long time. Forster excluded Ternan completely from his *Life of Dickens*, and other confidants, like Wilkie Collins and W. H. Wills, were impressively loyal in their silence about Dickens' affair. Ternan herself also kept the secret, denying that she had been Dickens' mistress. She even withheld it from her children, who did not know until after she died that their mother shared years of her life with one of the most famous Victorians. Ternan's discretion certainly helped to protect her own reputation, but, on top of the silence of all the others who knew about the affair, it also testifies to the force of Dickens' influence. His desire to manage his own legacy was intense, and other people's desire to satisfy Dickens' wishes was obviously strong enough to silence them about the most intriguing aspect of his life.

In a way, Dickens even tried to silence himself. In 1860, he made a huge bonfire at Gad's Hill into which he threw all his correspondence. He asked his friends to burn their letters from him (many did not heed his orders) and had smaller fires in later years to continue the erasure. Indeed, for decades, the relationship between Dickens and Ternan was not publicly known at all. Once scholars began unearthing its details in the twentieth century, they caused a scandal of their own. Admirers of Dickens were outraged at suggestions that he had been adulterous and that unsavoury elements of his life conflicted so drastically with the world they saw in his novels. As Dickens had wished, his version of the marital separation had gone fairly unquestioned in the writing of his history, and his voice clearly dominated Catherine's (Nelly's being wholly absent). The 1860 bonfire, however, only fanned the flames of curiosity for future chroniclers of his life. Rather than laying speculation to rest, the remaining evidence (in both Dickens' writings and others') has led to more rather than less questioning about his affairs and a persistent interest in answering the questions that remain.

Just as Dickens could not get Ellen Ternan out of his mind after the Manchester performances of *The Frozen Deep*, the play's plot and characters also lingered in his mind, inspiring his next novel. Dickens was so moved by his own portrayal of Richard Wardour that he used the idea of self-sacrifice in the name of love to develop the character of Sydney Carton in *A Tale of Two Cities*, which appeared in *All the Year Round* from 30th April to 26th November 1859. *All the Year Round* built upon the success of *Household Words* by increasing the number of serialised novels it published. Works like Wilkie Collins' sensational *The Woman in White*, which immediately followed *A Tale of Two Cities*, were extremely popular, helping *All the Year Round* to more than double the circulation numbers of *Household Words*. For the early issues, Dickens used it strategically as the vehicle for his own new novel in order to boost sales, even though he knew from experience that the pressure of writing for weekly rather than monthly instalments would be exhausting. The rush of producing weekly instalments was appropriate, however, for a novel full of travel and haste. Its characters move between England and France, incarceration and freedom. Rebellious crowds surge and march. Lovers are caught in suspenseful flights toward and away from the guillotine. History itself moves back and forth, as characters must pay for the sins of the past in order for the future to change. Choosing the French Revolution during the Reign of Terror as his setting, Dickens returned to the historical novel mode he first attempted in *Barnaby Rudge* with much more success. While *A Tale of Two Cities* shares *Rudge*'s concern with mobs and riots, its relatively short length and poignant romance plot made it far more popular with readers, who were simultaneously saddened and uplifted by Sydney Carton's choice to give his life so that the woman he loves may find happiness. *A Tale of Two Cities* offered a change from Dickens' recent fiction, not only in its historical setting, but also in characterisation. Dickens pulled away from the psychology of his characters, spending far less time investigating their interiority, which led some reviewers (then and now) to complain about the book's superficiality. Others have noted that the novel's refusal to grant access to its characters' interior lives points toward its larger theme that human beings are always closed to one another.

In the year after the publication of *A Tale of Two Cities*, Dickens was restless and melancholy. He experienced a series of domestic losses: Katey married, his brother Alfred died and he sold his London house. He wrote several essays for *All the Year Round* between January and October of 1860 that featured lonely urban walks and visits to the Paris Morgue to stare at the bodies of the dead. *Great Expectations* took shape during this gloomy time. It is a book dominated by partings (one of its favourite words) and preoccupied with frustrated rather than fulfilled love. Dickens approached characterisation very differently than he had in his previous novel. Instead of skimming the surface, he wrote a first-person narrative that conveys great interior depth. Following Pip from boy to manhood, we see a protagonist who is far more fallible and disappointing than many of Dickens' previous heroes. Pip, a boy apprenticed to be a blacksmith, aspires to become a gentleman and receives an unexpected fortune from an unknown benefactor. Pip assumes that his patron is the wealthy Miss Havisham and that he is destined for her lovely ward, Estella, but he learns painfully that his true patron is an escaped convict he once helped when he was a small boy. Indeed, Pip finds that he has habitually misread his life, mistaking snobbery for gentlemanly behaviour and confusing cruelty with love. His 'expectations' are continually thwarted, and his relationship with Estella shows how disturbed childhoods produce multi-dimensional adults whose complex motivations often result in behaviours that do them more harm than good. *Great Expectations* also features one of Dickens' most memorable characters. Literally encrusted in her wedding gown since she was jilted by her fiancé, surrounded by rotting party food and stopped clocks, Miss Havisham twists Estella into her instrument of retribution against the male sex, leading her into an abusive marriage and breaking Pip's heart in the process. Although the novel's final chapter holds out the faint possibility that Pip and Estella might recover personally and even romantically, it refuses to end conclusively. Its ambiguity is also the result of significant and unusual revision. In an unprecedented move, Dickens completely changed the ending after showing his first draft to Edward Bulwer-Lytton, who wanted a happier conclusion for Pip. Much debate has ensued about just how much happier the published ending is, and Dickens complicated the whole issue further by changing the final line yet again in a later edition. Whether or not Pip and Estella ever truly part is never fully resolved. *Great Expectations* was serialised in *All the Year Round* from 1st December 1860 to 3rd August 1861, and, despite its success, the public had to wait almost three years for its successor.

For Dickens now began to withdraw from public view. One of the most perplexing periods in his life is from 1862 to 1865. With the exception of a few readings in Paris in January of 1863, Dickens stopped his performances from January 1862 to April 1866. He had no novels in print from the end of 1861 to May 1864

– just the journalism and Christmas numbers in *All the Year Round*. During this period, Dickens also took unusually frequent trips to France. In the summer of 1862, he was alarmed by Georgina's development of what seemed to be heart problems, so he brought her to France with him for a short time. Her swift recovery by the autumn and the inconsistent reasons Dickens gave in his letters for his trips abroad have led many to believe that Georgina's illness may have simply been distress related to a problem with Ternan. (The same heart condition that killed Mary Hogarth did eventually resurface in the family, killing Dickens' son Walter suddenly in India on the last day of 1863.) Intriguingly, there is no record at all of Ellen Ternan's life from 1862 to 1865. None of her letters exist from that time, no evidence of where she was living has been found and she and her mother did not attend her sister Maria's wedding in 1863. These are the years in which many have suggested that Ellen and Mrs Ternan were living in France and that Ellen gave birth to an infant who did not survive.

The assertion that Dickens and Ternan had a child is controversial because it cannot be substantiated with definitive proof. It is not a possibility that can be dismissed hastily, however. Dickens' many references to a continuing crisis and a sick friend in his letters from this time are suggestive of a Ternan pregnancy. Additional strong pieces of evidence come from two of Dickens' own children: Katey and Henry. Gladys Storey recorded Katey saying that Dickens and Ternan had a son who died. Storey also cited a conversation with Henry in 1928 in which he referred to a dead son of Charles and Ellen. There seems to be no reason why two of Dickens' children, especially two with whom he was very close, would fabricate a story about a dead illegitimate sibling. At the end of her life, Katey's stated wish was for Storey to write an accurate book about her father's life, and given that Henry had gone out of his way to publicly disprove a patently bogus claim in 1908 that Dickens had fathered a son by Georgina, it is especially unconvincing to think that he would perpetuate a lie about Ellen. At the very least, Katey's and Henry's statements show that they took for granted that the relationship between their father and Ellen Ternan was both romantic and sexual. The credibility of these reports rests largely upon how one views Storey's account, and, again, it is difficult to find a convincing explanation for why she would invent such a scenario. Some have suggested that Dickens' relationship with Ternan was more paternal than sexual. While Nelly being the same age as Katey certainly introduces the father–daughter comparison, a twenty-seven-year age difference does not cancel out the potential for erotic desire, especially since men routinely married women decades their junior in this period. It also seems implausible to propose that a man who fathered ten children (not counting at least two miscarriages) in sixteen years would abruptly lose his sexual appetite when he began spending most of his time with a beautiful young woman. Unless new evidence is uncovered, it remains an intriguing if contested possibility that Dickens fathered a child with Ternan.

Whether or not they were recovering from the recent birth and loss of a child, the Dickens–Ternan relationship narrowly escaped its own death and came frighteningly close to widespread exposure on 9th June 1865 as Mrs Ternan, Nelly and Charles were travelling from Paris back to London. At full speed, their train was approaching a bridge in Staplehurst, Kent when a railway worker suddenly flagged for the driver to brake because some rails had been removed from the track for repair work. The signal came too late. The front of the train dramatically leapt the bridge, but most of the carriages careened off the tracks. Dickens' party avoided life-threatening injury because their first-class carriage was far enough forward to dangle on the hillside rather than plunging downward onto the river bank. It is not entirely clear how much time Dickens spent tending to Nelly's injuries (in future letters, he refers to her as 'The Patient' and calls Mrs Ternan an 'older woman' in their carriage), but he quickly tried to help the other passengers whose carriages had fared worse than his own. Multiple accounts describe Dickens using his hat and brandy flask to carry water to the crash victims, some of whom died as he was trying to save them. In all, ten people died, and scores more were seriously injured. Dickens refused to appear at the inquest, where he would have had to name his fellow travellers, but he was bold enough to enquire after Nelly's lost jewellery, some of which had personal engravings. The accident traumatised Dickens for the rest of his life: he felt nervous in railway carriages and coaches alike, rattled by the thought of another disaster.

Ellen's jewellery was not the only item Dickens attempted to rescue from the destroyed train car. He also climbed back into the precarious wreckage to retrieve the manuscript of his latest novel, *Our Mutual Friend*, which was published between May 1864 and November 1865. It is appropriate, then, that Dickens' last completed work is preoccupied with resurrection. The novel describes a modern urban setting dominated by heaps of city garbage containing buried treasures waiting to be unearthed. Throughout the narrative, these 'Dust Mounds' are a constant reminder of life's redemptive possibilities, and more than one character is pulled from the baptismal depths to live again. The opening chapter features Lizzie Hexam and her father dredging the Thames for bodies, and the novel is punctuated by several near drownings. But not everyone who receives a second chance deserves it. The moral ambivalence of this novel is a far cry from the melodramatic clarity of Dickens' earlier fiction, which draws an extreme contrast between its heroes and villains and rewards and punishes each accordingly. In *Our Mutual Friend*, Dickens allows the dissipated and aristocratic Eugene Wrayburn to marry the working-class girl he almost ruins, and he instantly reconciles another wife, Bella Wilfer, to the idea that her husband has deliberately married her under false pretences. Nor does human frailty necessarily lead to the painful loss of *Great Expectations*, which eschews a conventionally happy ending for its protagonist. *Our Mutual Friend*, by contrast, marries off its romantic couples. This may account for the subtle sense of unease that permeates the novel's final chapters. Dickens strains to maintain a happy ending, which avows that Bella maintain 'perfect faith' in her husband despite his months of deceit. The novel ultimately closes not on a scene of married life but on two bachelors, contented enough but forever excluded from the domestic bonds that the book strives to endorse.

Now fifty-three years of age, Dickens continued to approach life with his customary energy and drive. Staplehurst had shown Dickens how dangerous railway travel was, but it did not stop him from using the trains on an almost daily basis at the end of his life. He installed Nelly at a cottage in Slough, apparently using the alias Charles Tringham (and variations on Tringham) to pay the rent, and later moved her to Windsor Lodge in Peckham, both locations easy to reach by several trains and far more convenient than France. His routine was to divide his time between Gad's Hill and Nelly's place of residence when he was not doing readings, although on numerous occasions he sent notes of apology to Georgina at Gad's Hill because he chose to spend extra time away. At times, Dickens was bold enough to have Nelly in the audience for his readings, and she was on friendly terms with Georgina and Dickens' friends even though she could never make proper visits to Gad's Hill (after his death, she remained in touch with both Georgina and Mamie). While Dickens revelled in the constant motion of his life, it began to take its toll on him physically. He had been plagued with foot problems for years, which he called 'neuralgia' because he refused to accept a diagnosis of gout, and, as he grew older, his left foot was increasingly painful and swollen.

Despite his failing health, and against the advice of his doctors, Dickens was determined to take another trip to America for a reading tour. He wanted Nelly to accompany him, but because of her own health or concerns about publicity, it was not feasible for her to join him on his initial crossing. She went to Italy with her family, and he set up a system whereby he would send a coded telegram with instructions on whether or not she was to join him. Wills was the conduit for the telegram and Dickens' letters to her, and Forster also was made responsible for taking care of any of Ternan's needs during Dickens' absence. It is unclear if Nelly was more inclined to go to America or to remain with her family (relations between Fanny Ternan and Dickens had cooled since her marriage to Thomas Trollope), but Dickens' telegram indicated that Nelly should not come. From November 1867 to April 1868, Dickens stayed in America alone. For all his weakness and discomfort, the tour was another great success. On New Year's Eve 1867, Mark Twain saw Dickens read in New York, and in his January 1868 submission to the San Francisco *Daily Alta California* he described him as

a tall, 'spry,'... thin-legged old gentleman, gotten up regard-less of expense, especially as to shirt-front and diamonds, with a bright red flower in his button-hole, gray beard and moustache, bald head, and... side hair brushed fiercely and tempestuously forward, as if its owner were sweeping down before a gale of wind... That fashion he has of brush-ing his hair and goatee so resolutely forward gives him a comical Scotch-terrier look about the face, which is rather heightened than otherwise by his portentous dignity and gravity.

This is a striking portrait of the ailing yet still impressive fifty-five-year-old Dickens.

Overall, this trip to America and the big cities of the East coast was much more pleasant than the visit Dickens and Catherine had shared over twenty years previously. Dickens even met President Andrew Johnson in February, just before the leader was impeached. The notes that he wrote to Wills (which accom-panied his letters for Ternan) and the accounts of some of his hosts, though, show that he was pining for his 'Darling', Nelly, and anxious to return to her. There is also the possibility that

Nelly was dealing with another pregnancy during his absence. After the deaths of Wills and Dickens, the managers of Wills' estate said that they gave letters with instructions from Dickens about a woman's confinement to Henry Dickens, and Storey noted that Katey and Henry each read the letters before burning them.

When Dickens returned to England in April of 1868, Nelly was back from Italy to meet him, and he spent a week with her before going to Gad's Hill. By the autumn, he was back into his routine of giving public readings and spending the rest of his time at Gad's Hill or Nelly's residence in Peckham. In November, he added a powerful piece to his repertoire when he began reading the account of Bill Sikes' murder of Nancy in *Oliver Twist*. By all accounts, this reading was disturbing, riveting and certain to bring the audience to tears. The violence Nancy suffers was not only felt by the audience. Again, Dickens was physically weakened by the intensity of his performance, and his friends and doctors pleaded with him to stop. In April of 1869, they finally prevailed, but only after Dickens had suffered a mild stroke. The incident forced Dickens into enough awareness of his mortality for him to write his will the following month. Still, he was forward-looking enough later in the summer to begin a new novel, *The Mystery of Edwin Drood*. This work undoubtedly lives up to its title; the mystery will remain because Dickens did not live long enough to finish it.

Dickens planned that *The Mystery of Edwin Drood* should be published in twelve instalments rather than the usual twenty, but he completed only the first six. John Jasper, Dickens' final protagonist and the main suspect in the murder of the title character, is both an upstanding member of the community and a frustrated opium addict. Many have noted that Jasper may echo Dickens' own divided self and that Ellen Lawless Ternan's name seems only slightly disguised as Helena Landless in the book. No letters or records definitively determine how Dickens was going to conclude the novel, but that has not stopped aficionados from penning their own endings and scrutinising the illustrations on the cover wrapper to guess at what he had in mind. The man who delighted for over forty years in engaging with the Victorian reading public – but also keeping them in the dark about so many things – left them in the midst of a mystery.

Right up to the end of his life, Dickens had maintained a full and demanding schedule. As 1870 began, he was working on *The Mystery of Edwin Drood*, which began its serialisation in April, as well as completing a series of farewell readings in London from January to March. His final performance, on 15th March, drew thunderous cheers and ovations that overwhelmed Dickens with emotion. On 9th March he had enjoyed a private audience with Queen Victoria, during which the two exchanged compliments. Katey and Mamie worried about how much their father's writing was taxing him, and the whole family was aware of his deteriorating condition, but Dickens lived his final week as he had lived his whole life: busy. He spent a late night at the offices of *All the Year Round*, kept up his walks around Gad's Hill and worked for more hours than usual on the novel. He went out of his way, staying up late into the night, to have a long talk with Katey about her future, and she recalled an unusually warm embrace from him as she and Mamie departed for London on Monday, 6th June. On 8th June, after a full day of writing, a stroke caused Dickens to collapse at dinner. He never regained consciousness and died the following day, on 9th June 1870.

Dickens' dead body lay at Gad's Hill, but, as with so many things in the final years of his life, there is some ambiguity about how, when and in what state the body arrived. The generally accepted story is that Dickens collapsed at Gad's Hill with Georgina, who then sent for Mamie, Katey, Charley, and eventually Ellen Ternan. However, the descendants of Revd Postans, who became the minister of a church in Peckham in 1872, have shared letters that suggest an alternative possibility. The letters relate the story of an old caretaker who said he secretly helped to transport the dead or dying Dickens from Windsor Lodge, where he was with Nelly, to Gad's Hill. To avoid scandal, Nelly and Georgina presumably then agreed on a more palatable story for the public. Whether Dickens' last conscious moments were spent with Georgina or Nelly, he was with a woman he cherished. Both women were ideals of youth, beauty and grace to him. One chose to be a mother figure for his children and to run his household even after an ugly marital separation. The other chose to respond to his love by passing her youth in a secret relationship. Both endured scandalous rumours about their intimacies with Dickens, and each was wife-like in her own way. That these two women should be together with Dickens' corpse, managing the manner in which his death was presented to the public, was fitting. They knew all too well how important the presentation and narrative of the event was to a world so interested in Dickens, and to the man himself.

Dickens liked to have the last word, and, while he was not able to conclude *The Mystery of Edwin Drood*, he did try to write the end to his own story in his last will and testament. It is a fascinating and somewhat surprising document. Its first sentence blatantly names Ellen Ternan in the way Dickens had avoided for so long in his letters, leaving her £1,000. This unexpected and extremely public acknowledgment of her can be read in multiple ways. Was Dickens finally trying to show her respect by admitting that she was the woman uppermost in his mind and thoughts, or was this an irresponsible act that put the reputation she and Dickens had spent so many years guarding at risk? One thousand pounds was a lot of money, but, given the size of Dickens' estate, it was not much, and it certainly would not have left Ellen secure for life. Many have speculated that Dickens made other, more discreet arrangements (mentioned obliquely in letters to Forster) for her lifetime settlement. In addition to naming Ellen, Dickens also used his will to take one more posthumous jab at Catherine. After imploring his children to honour Georgina as a mother figure, he wrote,

And I desire here simply to record the fact that my wife, since our separation by consent, has been in the receipt from me of an annual income of £600, while all the great charges of a numerous and expensive family have devolved wholly upon myself.

Even in death, Dickens was unable to address Catherine kindly. Not all others followed suit. Although Catherine was not invited to Dickens' funeral, Queen Victoria sent a note of condolence to her, and she ended up visiting Charley and her grandchildren regularly at Gad's Hill – an arrangement that would probably have driven Dickens to distraction.

Catherine's ability to recapture a certain status as his widow is just one example of how, with the exception of financial matters, many did not grant authority to Dickens' voice in the will. The document, in a tone that nearly shouts, states, 'I emphatically direct that I be buried in an inexpensive, unostentatious, and strictly private manner.' In typical fashion, Dickens even describes what his mourners should and should not wear. Nevertheless, his family saw no use in opposing the entire country's desire for him to be honoured with a tomb alongside other literary giants in Westminster Abbey, where he was buried on 14th June 1870. In this act, his fans' wishes dominated his own, and the burial was an immediate signal that the public felt a strong right to participate in Dickens' memorialisation. Whether he liked it or not, his legacy would take on a life of its own.

Afterlife

One of the most touching and enduring tributes to Dickens is a drawing by Sir Samuel Luke Fildes, who had been working closely with Dickens on the illustrations for *The Mystery of Edwin Drood*. Fildes' watercolour, 'The Empty Chair', portrays Dickens' study exactly as he had left it: with the chair slightly pushed back from a most tidy desk. An engraving of the painting appeared in the 1870 Christmas number of *The Graphic*, and print reproductions of it remain popular to this day. The image, made at Gad's Hill right after the funeral, in many ways symbolises Dickens' legacy: he is gone, yet not gone. His empty chair, pulled out rather than pushed conclusively against the desk, points to his ghostly presence, now at large as an inspiration for other artists and writers. The books that line the shelves of his study remind us of generations of readers to come. Dickens is still an enormously popular author; his stories and characters remain recognisable to a large portion of the general public. Adaptations of his work abound on the stage, in print and on the large screen of the cinema as well as the small screen of the television. It is not an overstatement to say that Dickens is constantly remembered.

Dickens actually disliked ostentatious memorials. For a man who was proud of his celebrity, this may seem odd, but it fits his lifelong pattern of courting fame while fiercely protecting his privacy. His will states:

I conjure my friends on no account to make me the subject of any monument, memorial, or testimonial whatever. I rest my claims to the remembrance of my country upon my published works, and to the remembrance of my friends upon their experience of me in addition thereto.

Despite this request, nearly a quarter of a century later, Dickens' global appeal won out. In 1894, the organisers of the Chicago World's Fair commissioned Frank Elwell to create a life-sized bronze statue of Dickens. Elwell's striking design features Little Nell looking up at a towering Dickens seated above her on a pedestal. The fair's directors shipped the statue to England as a gift, but Henry Dickens and other family members so strongly opposed its existence that it was ultimately returned to America without even being unpacked. It eventually found a home in Philadelphia's Clark Park where it continues to stand as confirmation of Dickens' posthumous reputation, which far exceeds the boundaries of his native country. It remains the only life-sized statue of Dickens in the world, but smaller memorials containing his image in the form of mugs, shirts and scores of other small paraphernalia can be found worldwide.

While he may have failed in discouraging any monuments or memorials, the second part of Dickens' wish – that his published works be his main claim to remembrance – has certainly been granted. Alongside William Shakespeare, Charles Dickens is one of the most familiar names in literary history. There was a lull in the academic study of Dickens in the late-nineteenth and early-twentieth centuries, when his massive popularity actually worked against him in circles that opposed 'popular' literature in favour of a more elitist notion of 'high' art. By the end of the nineteenth century, some readers regarded Dickens as bulky and overly sentimental. Oscar Wilde, for instance, is reputed to have once remarked that 'One must have a heart of stone to read the death of Little Nell without laughing'. By the mid-twentieth century, however, scholars began to rediscover the thematic complexity and aesthetic merit of Dickens' work, and today his position as one of the most important novelists in history is secure. New book-length studies, companions, indexes and essay collections are published each year. Increasing interest in his journalism has led to the publication of new editions of the pieces that Dickens wrote for his own as well as other periodicals, and the digitisation of *Household Words* and *All the Year Round* will ensure that more scholars than ever before have access to a relatively under-examined set of Dickens texts. Fresh theories, readings and appreciations of this aspect of Dickens' work are sure to come.

Dickens has also had a long-lasting impact on the genre of the novel itself. He developed this literary form so vividly and powerfully that other writers have, like the Artful Dodger, been picking his pocket for the past two hundred years. A long list of authors – including Catherine Cookson, Michael Faber, Sheri Holman, Charles Palliser and Sarah Waters – have not only imitated Dickens' style, but also self-consciously borrowed or played with his plot devices, characters and settings. Other novelists have 'talked back' to individual Dickens novels more pointedly. *Great Expectations* alone has inspired multiple rewrites and retellings, from Kathy Acker's 1983 *Great Expectations*, which borrows the novel's opening paragraph, to Peter Carey's *Jack Maggs* (1999), which recasts Magwitch, the convict, as the true hero of the book. Dickens may not have wanted a memorial, but the persistent intertextual conversation he inspired testifies to the enduring importance of his fiction to other writers who are so awed, irritated or intimidated by his work that they revisit it in their own novels.

Perhaps because his fiction was integrated into the colonial educational system, V.S. Naipaul, Salman Rushdie, Wole Soyinka, Michelle Cliff and many other writers from former British colonies also cite the impact of Dickens on their lives and work. Lloyd Jones's *Mister Pip* (2006) shows this education at work in his novel about a group of students living in

Bougainville during the 1990s revolution. They are so invested in *Great Expectations* that when their only copy of the book is lost, they invent the rest of it themselves. For postcolonial authors, Dickens is a conflicted symbol. On one hand, as someone who endorsed the Empire and wrote some troubling racial stereotypes, such as 'the Native' in *Dombey and Son*, whose endurance of verbal and physical abuse is described in disturbingly comic terms, Dickens represents colonial authority. On the other hand, his work also advocates resistance to oppression, and his fiction reveals a keen awareness of the painful impact of social origins on identity. His novels, so often held up in the colonies as quintessentially English and thus worthy of admiration and even sometimes memorisation, inspire profoundly mixed reactions: disavowal, love, ambivalence, resistance and, finally, interrogation. As Indo-Guyanese Canadian Cyril Dabydeen says in his poem 'Fagin and Me', 'I encountered Fagin in a far place, / and asked, "You, what can you tell me?"' But even postcolonial denunciations of Dickens implicitly acknowledge Dickens' importance by making him the target of their resistance. His fiction has been fully – if sometimes uneasily – integrated into global culture.

Intertextual conversations on Dickens extend well beyond the novel. In fact, as the Russian film director Sergei Eisenstein famously remarked, Dickens seems to have been made for film. Eisenstein's ground-breaking analysis of Dickens' impact on cinema observes that early filmmakers like D. W. Griffith learned much about their craft from paying attention to Dickens' technique: his rendering of dynamic urban spaces; his close-up takes of small, intimate details; his cross cutting between plots; and his use of montage. The very first feature films made in Britain adapted either Shakespeare or Dickens, not only because their respective styles lent themselves to film, but also because both authors were considered so fundamentally important to English culture that adaptations of their work helped to legitimise the new technology. Some of the most influential films in the history of cinema, such as David Lean's *Great Expectations* (1946), have been adaptations of Dickens' novels. Lean's film has inspired everyone from Alfonso Cuarón, who made his own version of *Great Expectations* in 1998 starring Ethan Hawke and Gwyneth Paltrow, to the creators of the television show *South Park*, who spoofed Lean's film in an episode from November of 2000. Early film versions of *Oliver Twist*, *David Copperfield*, *A Tale of Two Cities* and *Great Expectations* have fundamentally shaped the development of both English and American cinema.

The Dickens work that has been adapted more than any other is *A Christmas Carol*, endlessly reincarnated in film, television and the theatre. The hundreds of adaptations have cemented Dickens' appeal to every generation since his own and ensured that he remains a household name. From children's cartoon versions to extravagant musicals, new versions of the story appear again and again. Ebenezer Scrooge has been played not only by veteran actors like Albert Finney, George C. Scott and Alastair Sim, but also by soap opera stars and even pop divas, possibly because Scrooge's transformation into a friendlier person makes the role a perfect vehicle for celebrities eager to make their public images seem less remote. It has become virtually obligatory for serial television programmes to produce a *Carol* episode every December. Although viewers may groan when a favourite cast member predictably develops Scrooge-like characteristics, each unimaginative adaptation is matched by a surprise like Walt Disney's *Mickey's Christmas Carol* (1983), which features a spot-on Scrooge McDuck, or a wittily satirical film like *Scrooged* (1988), set in a television studio making an adaptation of *A Christmas Carol*. Indeed, *A Christmas Carol* is so ubiquitous that Scrooge has been transformed from a proper name to a general noun ('don't be a scrooge') and even a verb, as above.

But if most of Dickens' works have been adapted for television or the cinema, then *A Christmas Carol* is the exception to that trend, for it appears with far more frequency on the stage, particularly in America. American regional theatres, which do not usually have the benefit of the state financial assistance received by many of their European counterparts, often schedule *A Christmas Carol* with the assumption that it will bring in enough revenue to fund their less traditional programming. Annual resurrections take almost every form imaginable, from 'straight' versions that feature a Dickensian narrator to spoofs and parodies (the latter of which usually stop short of cynically flouting Dickens' vision of human compassion and social unification). The story has been recast in a variety of different settings, transposed to the queer New York scene of the nineties (with Scrooge as an old queen) to the American old West (with Scrooge as an old cowboy) to the contemporary urban ghetto (with Scrooge as a loan shark). While these revised settings are often intended for comic effect, some move away from nineteenth-century England in order to comment sharply on contemporary social conditions, thus working toward the kind of social progress for which Dickens yearned. One of the most well-known stage versions of *A Christmas Carol* in recent memory is Patrick Stewart's one-man show, which debuted in 1993. Virtuoso performances like Stewart's capture the essence of Dickens' public readings while small regional productions echo the kind of collaborative Christmas storytelling that Dickens enjoyed so much in the annual Christmas numbers. Much of Dickens' work has appeared on the stage at one point or another. There are not only numerous plays based on his novels, but also some featuring Dickens himself, such as Peter Ackroyd's and Simon Callow's *The Mystery of Charles Dickens* (2002). *A Christmas Carol*, however, remains the work most intimately associated with the theatre.

Dickens also surfaces in music, from the band named after Uriah Heep to the Dickens-inspired narrators of The Decemberists to the contemporary rap scene. The world of rap and hip hop music may seem an unlikely area of culture in which to find Dickens, but his presence there actually illuminates the

ongoing power of his commitment to social reform. In addition
to rappers like Ludacris and Kanye West, the internationally
popular rap artist Jay-Z has referenced Dickens more than once.
The horrible living conditions, general danger and child exploita-
tion of modern, poverty-stricken urban landscapes are not all
that different from Fagin's den in *Oliver Twist* or the unforgiving
streets Jo wanders in *Bleak House*. Jay-Z's 1999 song 'Anything',
for instance, features a fascinating twice removed echo of
Dickens. A guest track on Beanie Siegel's *The Truth* (1999), the
song's chorus samples Lionel Bart's musical *Oliver!*, the film
version of which won the Academy Award for Best Picture in
1968. Jay-Z raps primarily about solidarity among men in the
ghetto, addressing his 'nephews' and explicitly envisioning himself as a father or uncle figure for African American young men
who have been orphaned by their fathers. This concern with
orphans, in addition to an emphasis on camaraderie, loyalty and
rebellion against the authorities, is appropriately Dickensian.

If Dickens' plots, themes and characters have made their way
out into the world at large, then the reverse is also true: there
is more than one organisation that promises to bring real-life visitors into Dickens' world for research or for profit. For research,
there is the 'Dickens Universe' hosted by the Dickens Project at
The University of California Santa Cruz. A scholarly consortium
founded in 1981, the Dickens Universe annually brings together
members of the general public, students and educators from the
primary all the way to the university level for an intensive week-
long study of Dickens' work. For profit, there is Dickens World,
opened in May of 2007 in Chatham Maritime, Kent. The Dickens
Fellowship advised on historical and fictional details, and the
park promises that visitors will be 'immersed in the urban
streets, sounds and smells of the 19th century'. One wonders
exactly how desirable it would be to be greeted with truly
authentic 'smells', since the urban centres of Dickens' actual
world did not enjoy adequate sewage or waste treatment. There
is a Great Expectations Boat Ride, which shows its passengers

rooftops as well as sewers, and a Scrooge-themed haunted house introduces its guests to dead characters from several of Dickens' stories. 'Naughty delights' are said to greet patrons at the Victorian Music Hall, and child care is available at 'Fagin's Den'. Predictably, some have complained that the park dilutes the intensity of Dickens' social critique, pleas for reform and sharp-edged humour. Others feel that Dickens himself would have loved its showmanship and that its popular (though expensive) appeal is consistent with his love of celebrity.

The adaptation of Dickens' work, sometimes into bizarre and fantastic new forms, testifies to its endurance almost two hundred years after his birth. The Dickens who appears to us today – in the classroom, in literary criticism, on the stage or in film, in music or in a theme park – may not be quite the same Dickens read by his Victorian contemporaries. Even the single-volume novels sold in bookstores remove us from the experience of reading nineteenth-century serial fiction. Yet he is not unrecognisable, and his work continues to resonate in the contemporary world. As the bicentennial of Dickens' birth approaches, his afterlife shows no sign of waning.

Selected works

1836 *Sketches by Boz* (First Series, 8th February. Second Series
17th December)
The Pickwick Papers (April 1836 – November 1837)
1837 *Oliver Twist* (February 1837 – April 1839 in *Bentley's Miscellany*)
1838 *Memoirs of Joseph Grimaldi* (February)
Nicholas Nickleby (April 1838 – October 1839)
1840 *Sketches of Young Couples* (10th February)
The Old Curiosity Shop (25th April 1840 – 6th February 1841
in *Master Humphrey's Clock*)
1841 *Barnaby Rudge* (13th February – 27th November in *Master
Humphrey's Clock*)
1842 *American Notes* (18th October)
1843 *Martin Chuzzlewit* (January 1843 – July 1844)
A Christmas Carol (19th December)
1844 *The Chimes* (16th December)
1845 *The Cricket on the Hearth* (20th December)
1846 *Pictures from Italy* (21st January – 2nd March in *The Daily News*)
Dombey and Son (October 1846 – April 1848)
1848 *The Haunted Man* (19th December)
1849 *David Copperfield* (May 1849 – November 1850)
1850 *Household Words* (30th March 1850 – 28th May 1859)
1851 *A Child's History of England* (January 1851 – 10th December 1853
in *Household Words*)
1852 *Bleak House* (March 1852 – September 1853)
1854 *Hard Times* (1st April – 12th August in *Household Words*)
1855 *Little Dorrit* (December 1855 – June 1857)
1859 *All the Year Round* (30th April 1859 – 1870)
A Tale of Two Cities (30th April – 26th November in *All the Year Round*)
1860 *The Uncommercial Traveller* (28th January 1860 – 24th July 1869 in
All the Year Round)
Great Expectations (1st December – 3rd August 1861 in *All the Year Round*)
1864 *Our Mutual Friend* (May 1864 – November 1865)
1870 *The Mystery of Edwin Drood* (1st April – September)

Collaborative Christmas Numbers

Household Words
1852 *A Round of Stories by the Christmas Fire*
1853 *Another Round of Stories by the Christmas Fire*
1854 *The Seven Poor Travellers*

1855 *The Holly-tree Inn*
1856 *The Wreck of the Golden Mary*
1857 *The Perils of Certain English Prisoners*
1858 *A House to Let*

All the Year Round
1859 *The Haunted House*
1860 *A Message from the Sea*
1861 *Tom Tiddler's Ground*
1862 *Somebody's Luggage*
1863 *Mrs Lirriper's Lodgings*
1864 *Mrs Lirriper's Legacy*
1865 *Doctor Marigold's Prescriptions*
1866 *Mugby Junction*
1867 *No Thoroughfare*

Bibliography

Ackroyd, Peter, *Dickens: A Biography* (London, 1990).

Andrews, Malcolm, *Charles Dickens and His Performing Selves: Dickens and the Public Readings* (Oxford, 2006).

Bodenheimer, Rosemarie, *Knowing Dickens* (Ithaca, 2007).

Bowen, John, *Other Dickens: Pickwick to Chuzzlewit* (Oxford, 2000).

Bowen, John, and Robert L. Patten, ed., *Palgrave Advances in Charles Dickens Studies* (Basingstoke, 2006).

Carey, John, *The Violent Effigy: A Study of Dickens' Imagination* (London, 1979).

Chesterton, G. K., *Charles Dickens* (London, 1906).

Collins, Philip Arthur William, *Dickens and Crime* (London, 1964).

Drew, John M. L., *Dickens the Journalist* (Basingstoke, 2003).

Forster, John, *The Life of Charles Dickens* (London, 1872–4).

House, Madeline, and Graham Storey, ed., *The Pilgrim Edition of The Letters of Charles Dickens*. 12 vols. (Oxford, 1965–2002).

Jacobson, Wendy S., ed., *Dickens and the Children of Empire* (Basingstoke, 2000).

John, Juliet, *Dickens's Villains: Melodrama, Character, Popular Culture* (Oxford, 2003).

Johnson, Edgar, *Charles Dickens: His Tragedy and Triumph*. 2 vols. (New York, 1952). 1 vol., revised and abridged (New York, 1977).

Jordan, John O., ed., *The Cambridge Companion to Charles Dickens* (Cambridge, 2001).

Kaplan, Fred, *Dickens: A Biography* (New York, 1988).

Kincaid, James R., *Dickens and the Rhetoric of Laughter* (Oxford, 1971).

Lester, Valerie Browne, *Phiz: The Man Who Drew Dickens* (London, 2006).

MacKay, Carol Hanbery, ed., *Dramatic Dickens* (Basingstoke, 1989).

Moore, Grace, *Dickens and Empire: Discourses of Class, Race and Colonialism in the Works of Charles Dickens* (Aldershot, 2004).

Nayder, Lillian, *Unequal Partners: Charles Dickens, Wilkie Collins, and Victorian Authorship* (London, 2002).

Newsom, Robert, *Dickens on the Romantic Side of Familiar Things: Bleak House and the Novel Tradition* (New York, 1977).

Nisbet, Ada, *Dickens and Ellen Ternan* (Berkeley, 1952).

Patten, Robert L, *Charles Dickens and His Publishers* (Oxford, 1978).

Sadrin, Anny, ed., *Dickens, Europe and the New Worlds* (Basingstoke, 1999).

Schlicke, Paul, ed., *Oxford Reader's Companion to Dickens* (Oxford, 1999).

Schor, Hilary, *Dickens and the Daughter of the House* (Cambridge, 1999).

Slater, Michael, *Charles Dickens* (Oxford, 2007); *Dickens and Women* (Stanford, 1983).

Smith, Grahame, *Dickens and the Dream of Cinema* (Manchester, 2003).

Stewart, Garrett, *Dickens and the Trials of Imagination* (Cambridge, Mass., 1974).

Stone, Harry, *The Night Side of Dickens: Cannibalism, Passion, Necessity* (Columbus, 1994).

Storey, Gladys, *Dickens and Daughter* (London, 1939).

Thomas, Deborah, *Dickens and the Short Story* (Philadelphia, 1982).

Tomalin, Claire, *The Invisible Woman: The Story of Ellen Ternan and Charles Dickens* (London, 1991).

Vlock, Deborah, *Dickens, Novel Reading, and the Victorian Popular Theatre* (Cambridge, 1998).

Waters, Catherine, *Dickens and the Politics of the Family* (Cambridge, 1997).

Welsh, Alexander, *The City of Dickens* (Cambridge, Mass., 1971); *From Copyright to Copperfield: The Identity of Dickens* (Cambridge, Mass., 1987).

Wilson, Edmund,. *The Wound and the Bow: Seven Studies in Literature* (Oxford, 1941).

Biographical note

Melissa Valiska Gregory is an Assistant Professor at the University of Toledo. Her book, *Domestic Terror in Victorian Culture*, is forthcoming from Ashgate Press. Melisa Klimaszewski is a Visiting Assistant Professor at DePauw University. She has published articles on Victorian servants and domesticity and has edited Hesperus' edition of Charles Dickens' *A Round of Stories by the Christmas Fire*. Together, Gregory and Klimaszewski have edited Hesperus editions of Charles Dickens' *Doctor Marigold's Prescriptions*, *Somebody's Luggage*, and *The Wreck of the Golden Mary*.

SELECTED TITLES FROM HESPERUS PRESS

Brief Lives

Author	Title
Richard Canning	*Brief Lives: Oscar Wilde*
Patrick Miles	*Brief Lives: Anton Chekhov*

Classics and Modern Voices

Author	Title	Foreword writer
Jane Austen	*Lesley Castle*	Zoë Heller
Mikhail Bulgakov	*The Fatal Eggs*	Doris Lessing
Joseph Conrad	*Heart of Darkness*	A.N. Wilson
Annie Dillard	*The Maytrees*	
Fyodor Dostoevsky	*The Gambler*	Jonathan Franzen
Thomas Hardy	*Wessex Poems*	Tom Paulin
Franz Kafka	*The Trial*	Zadie Smith
Georges Simenon	*Three Crimes*	
Leo Tolstoy	*Hadji Murat*	Colm Tóibín
Virginia Woolf	*The Platform of Time*